# TOP 10 CHICAGO

# CONTENTS

## 4

## Introducing Chicago



## 18

## Top 10 Highlights

46

## Top 10 of Everything



72

## Area by Area



108

## Streetsmart

# INTRODUCING CHICAGO



*Lincoln Park before Downtown*

# WELCOME TO **CHICAGO**

**Chicago is a second city in name only. It's a city overflowing with an array of things to do. In one day here, you can admire world-class art, summit skyscrapers, and enjoy live blues. Don't want to miss a thing? With Top 10 Chicago, you'll enjoy the very best the city has to offer.**

It's easy to see why millions of people take a trip to Chicago every year. Who could fail to be impressed by the city's signature skyscrapers, some of the first built in the world and, for a time, some of the tallest, too. There's the Willis Tower, with the highest observation deck in the country, and the John Hancock Center, with its 94th-floor glass observatory. Climbing to lofty heights in an entirely different way is the city's cultural scene. An entire trip could be spent admiring the Impressionist works at the Art Institute of Chicago, diving into culture and nature both old and new

**Skyscrapers along the river**

at the Field Museum, and engaging with interactive exhibits at the Griffin Museum of Science and Industry. And did we mention the music? Chicago is a world-renowned hub for blues and jazz. Come evening, the local bars reverberate to a sound and style that's only found here.

But as Jane Byrne, the city's first female mayor said, "Chicago's neighborhoods have always been the city's greatest strength." Spend some time exploring them and you'll understand why. From the Swedish heritage in Andersonville to the Mexican enclave of Pilsen, Greektown to LGBTQ+-friendly Northalsted, Chicago's 77 neighborhoods are a celebration of diversity and of the city's historical tradition of welcoming people from across the world. It's in these districts where the true soul of the city can be found. You'll taste it in the array of local eateries serving up Chicago staples and feel it at the city's many hallowed sporting stadiums, from Soldier Field to Wrigley Field, where locals of all backgrounds come together to holler for their heroes.

So, where to start? With Top 10 Chicago, of course. This pocket-sized guide gets to the heart of the city with simple lists of 10, expert local knowledge and comprehensive maps, helping you turn an ordinary trip into an extraordinary one.

# THE STORY OF **CHICAGO**

**The city of Chicago has come a long way since it was a frontier settlement. In the centuries inbetween, it's been ravaged by fire, shaped by pioneering architects, and been home to gangsters, cultural icons, and the first Black US president. Here's the story of how it came to be.**

## First Settlers

Before colonization, the Great Lakes region was heavily populated by many Indigenous groups, including the Iowa, Ho-Chunk, and Potawatomi, who had lived here for hundreds of years. Little is known about the area until the arrival of French explorers Lois Jolliet and Jacques Marquette, in 1673. In the century following these first arrivals, a steady stream of European explorers came to the area, yet none took steps to establish a permanent settlement. Instead, the first non-Indigenous resident was a Black freeman named Jean Baptiste Point du Sable, who set up a trading post in the 1780s. This was followed in 1804 by the construction of Fort Dearborn, built by the US Army. The fort was destroyed by Indigenous forces in the War of 1812 and rebuilt in 1816. Two years later, Illinois became a US state. Even after this, the area remained predominantly populated by Indigenous people, until the 1833 Treaty of Chicago forcibly removed most of these groups from the region.

## Early Chicago

Chicago's modern history really begins in the 1830s when it rapidly expanded and was given city status. By the 1840s, it was a key transport and trading hub thanks to the growth of the railroad and shipping, facilitated by major infrastructure projects that had connected the lakes with the Mississippi River. This growth meant Chicago was America's second-largest city by the 1860s. Then, disaster: over a period of 36 hours, the Great Chicago Fire of 1871 flattened an area 4-miles (6.5-km) long and 1-mile (2-km) wide, destroying some 18,000 buildings. More than 300 people died and a third of the population (about 100,000 people) were left homeless.

**European explorers meeting the Potawatomi people**

**The Masonic Temple skyscraper, designed by Daniel H. Burnham**

### Rebuilding and Social Justice

The ensuing reconstruction was both quick and dramatic. The downtown area was transformed by visionary architects, including Daniel H. Burnham and Louis Sullivan, who built offices, museums (such as the Art Institute of Chicago), and the world's first skyscrapers in 1885. The rapid rate of construction allowed the population to explode, rising from 500,000 in 1880 to 1.7 million in 1900.

But all was not well. Such growth put great pressure on the inadequate infrastructure, and the city was soon dealing with a public health crisis due to overcrowding and poor water quality in the Chicago River. Alongside these issues, workers also began to protest against long hours, hazardous conditions, and low wages. Strikes and riots occurred in 1873 and 1877, but these were mere precursors to the 1886 Haymarket Affair, when a bomb killed seven police officers at a peaceful demonstration. Four labor leaders were charged with murder and hanged despite very little evidence. The case garnered national media attention and cast Chicago in a bad light.

Yet, just four years later, the city was chosen to host the 1893 World's Columbian Exposition. The resulting six-month festival was a huge success, attracting 26 million visitors and transforming Chicago's reputation. Concerns over workers' rights were forgotten.

### Moments in History

**1673**
Frenchmen Louis Jolliet and Jacques Marquette are the first Europeans to reach the future Chicago area.

**1780s**
Jean Baptiste Point du Sable establishes Chicago's first permanent settlement near the mouth of the Chicago River.

**1833–1837**
Chicago experiences a rapid period of growth and is officially incorporated, first as a town and then a city.

**1871**
The Great Chicago Fire destroys most of the city, leaving thousands homeless.

**1893**
The World's Columbian Exposition (World's Fair) is held in Chicago, with many new buildings designed by architects such as Frank Lloyd Wright and Daniel H. Burnham.

**1919**
Riots starting in the South Side spark a summer of violence, now known the Chicago race riots.

**1960s**
The decade is marked by protests, both peaceful and violent, which culminate in the "Chicago Seven" trial and the murder of Black Panther Fred Hampton.

**1991–1998**
Michael Jordan leads the Chicago Bulls to six NBA titles within a decade.

**2008**
US President-elect and Chicago resident Barack Obama makes his victory speech in Grant Park.

**2019**
Lori Lightfoot becomes the first female Black mayor of Chicago.

**2025**
Chicago-born cardinal-bishop Robert Prevost is elected Pope Leo XIV.

## Boom and Bust

The city's population continued to expand during the early 20th century. Most migration had previously come from Europe, but as World War I made movement difficult, these migrants were replaced by increasing numbers of Black Americans from the South. They settled on the South Side, which became Chicago's first Black neighborhood and a de facto segregated area. The limited number of jobs and housing led to racial tensions, which bubbled over in the 1919 race riots, a summer of violence that killed 38 people.

The decades that followed were some of the most difficult in the city's history, and Chicago became synonymous with violence and political corruption. Gangsters like Al Capone brought barbarity to the city's streets, most infamously with the 1929 Valentine's Day Massacre. Budget mismanagement also meant Chicago was made virtually bankrupt by the Wall Street Crash of 1929. Despite public works projects and a second World's Fair, in 1933, the city could not avoid mass unemployment during the Great Depression. The economy floundered until World War II when Chicago's industrial base and workforce was put to use as part of the Allied war effort.

**Unemployed men queuing for food during the Great Depression**

**Barack Obama giving his 2008 election victory speech in Grant Park**

## Postwar Chicago

Chicago's economic recovery continued after the war. The city grew to 3.5 million people in 1950 and was a cultural hub, particularly for blues and jazz. However, as the 1950s wore on, industrial decline set in. Massive job losses occurred in several manufacturing industries and the city's population declined as many thousands moved away. What followed was a tumultous period defined by political activism, racial tensions, and a controversial mayor, Richard J. Daley (1955–1976). Daley gained notoriety for his approach to protests: first there was his heavy-handed response to the peaceful civil rights marches and the more violent uprisings that followed the assassination of Martin Luther King, Jr. in 1968; then there were the protests against the Vietnam War at the 1968 Democratic National Convention. Police beat unarmed protesters but it was the protesters who were famously taken to trial – the "Chicago Seven" made national (and international) news.

Controversial he may have been, but Daley remained very popular among locals. He oversaw the revival of central districts, attracted new businesses, and commissioned the Sears (now Willis) Tower in 1974, then the world's tallest building. His work was continued by his son Richard M. Daley, mayor from 1989 to 2011. Chicago also became fashionable during the 1980s and 90s thanks to a flourishing cultural and sporting scene: Chicago was the setting for many movies and both the Chicago Bears and Chicago Bulls won titles – the latter with arguably the most famous athlete in the world, Michael Jordan.

## Chicago Today

There is no doubt that Chicago is today one of the best cultural hubs in the US, with a plethora of world-class attractions. Mayors Rahm Emanuel and Lori Lightfoot have have opened up Chicago to new businesses and tourists through expanding downtown, investing in local projects, and improving infrastructure, most notably through renovating "L" stations and creating 200 miles (320 km) of bike paths.

But as history tells, the good comes with the bad. Chicago still suffers from high levels of inequality and poverty, and it has one of the highest murder rates in the US. Continued investment in social projects, community outreach, and rehabilitation programs for former inmates, are all essential to ensure a more hopeful future for all Chicagoans.

# TOP 10 EXPERIENCES

**Planning the perfect trip to Chicago? Whether you're visiting for the first time or making a return trip, there are some things you simply shouldn't miss out on. To make the most of your time – and to enjoy the very best this city has to offer – be sure to add these experiences to your list.**

## 1 Go on an architectural tour

Chicago was home to the world's first skyscraper and has seen plenty more since, designed by the likes of Daniel H. Burnham and Frank Lloyd Wright *(p49)*. See many of the best centrally-located towers in one trip on a cruise of the Chicago River with the Chicago Architecture Center *(p113)*.

## 2 Relax on lakeside beaches

It may be a surprise to learn that this Midwest city has over 25 miles (40 km) of pretty beaches on Lake Michigan. Take a break from sightseeing to kite-board on Montrose Beach *(p54)*, play volleyball on Oak Street Beach *(p54)*, or enjoy a sunset drink in Castaways Beach Club on North Avenue Beach *(p54)*.

## 3 Stroll the Magnificent Mile

Chicago has hundreds of attractions, but a whole trip could be spent in this 13-block stretch of North Michigan Avenue *(p40)*. Here, you'll find around 460 stores, 275 restaurants, and plenty of top sites including the Museum of Contemporary Art Chicago *(p83)* and the 100-story John Hancock Center *(p83)*.

## 4 Create a dining itinerary

From casual snack joints to world-class culinary institutions, Chicago has every type of eatery imaginable. Dine on dim sum and slurp down noodles in Chinatown *(p98)*, hit up the famous Mr. Beef *(p87)* to try its sandwiches, and, of course, make sure to try deep-dish pizza, found at pizzerias across the city.

## 5 Catch a game

This is a city that loves sport *(p71)*. Depending on when you visit, you could see the famous Bulls play basketball at the United Center *(p22)*, watch the Bears play an NFL game at Soldier Field *(p23)*, or see the Cubs play baseball at the iconic Wrigley Field *(p89)*.

## 6 Take in a museum

When it comes to museums, you're spoilt for choice. Headliners include the Art Institute of Chicago *(p24)* and the Field Museum *(p28)*, but there are plenty more besides, like the DuSable Black History Museum and Education Center *(p105)* and the Adler Planetarium *(p97)*.

## 7 Catch a comedy show

Chicago's comedy scene is world-famous. It was the birthplace of improv comedy and venues such as Second City *(p91)* and iO *(p64)* have launched the careers of many a star, from Bill Murray to Tina Fey. Today, the next generation of stars are sure to make you chuckle.

## 8 Go local

Chicago is more than just The Loop *(p74)*. It has 77 neighborhoods, each with their own flavor. Enjoy Mexican arts and culture in Pilsen *(p67)*, indulge in some high-end shopping in Lincoln Park *(p55)*, and explore the fascinating history of the Pullman area *(p57)*.

## 9 Listen to live music

Jazz and blues have long been an indelible part of the city's music scene. Today the best performers can be seen at local bars and historic venues such as Jazz Showcase *(p100)* and Blue Chicago *(p64)*. Look out for the city's blues and jazz festivals, too *(p70)*.

## 10 Take a walk in the park

Chicago has an incredible 600 parks, offering the perfect break from the urban bustle. Enjoy a lakeside stroll in Lincoln Park *(p55)*, catch a festival in Grant Park *(p23)*, or visit Millennium Park *(p42)* for its tranquil gardens, theaters, and unusual art installations.

# ITINERARIES

**Exploring the Magnificent Mile, eating deep-dish pizza, visiting the Museum Campus: there's a lot to see and do in Chicago. With places to eat, drink, or simply take in the view, these itineraries offer ways to spend 2 days and 4 days in the city.**

## 2 DAYS

### Day 1

#### Morning

Where better to spend your first day in Chicago than in the central Loop. Start your day in the bustling Millennium Park *(p42)*, home to many quirky installations. Visit the Frank Gehry-designed Jay Pritzker Pavilion, with its intertwined steel pipes, then head south to see the equally unusual Cloud Gate (known as "The Bean"), and the giant faces on the Crown Fountain screen. Just to the south is the Art Institute of Chicago *(p24)*, where you can spend the rest of the morning. There's much to see here so prioritize the collections you're most interested in. Beyond the Impressionist works, the American Gothic and Arts of Africa sections are worth checking out.

**EAT**

If you still have space around dinner on day 1, or lunch on day 2, take a break from sightseeing to visit the fun Museum of Ice Cream *(museumoficecream.com)*. As well as the exhibits, take advantage of the generous samples on offer.

**The exterior of the deep-dish specialists, Pizzeria Uno**

#### Afternoon

Enjoy lunch with city views at the rooftop restaurant of the Chicago Athletic Association *(p118)*, and then walk on to the American Writers Museum *(p79)*, which houses fascinating exhibits on America's literary tradition. From here, it's a short walk on Michigan Avenue to the Chicago River and the buzzing Riverwalk. Explore the area and hop aboard an architectural river cruise with First Lady Cruises *(p39)*, the best way to appreciate the city's designs. Cross the river for a dinner of deep-dish pizza at Pizzeria Uno *(p87)*. Nearby is the House of Blues *(houseofblues.com)* where you can extend your evening, listening to the unique Chicago blues sound.

### Day 2

#### Morning

Start your second day in the south of the city on the Museum Campus, which is home to several of Chicago's best attractions. Foremost among these is the Field Museum *(p28)*, where you can spend time delving into cultures from ancient Egypt to modern Africa. Or, if you prefer the natural world, visit SUE, the near-complete T-Rex skeleton, or the unique underground life of bugs exhibit. If you have time afterwards, the Adler Planetarium *(p97)* is worth a visit for its magical projection show and exhibits on astronomical discoveries. From here, take the Red "L" Line from Roosevelt to Jackson to reach the best view in the city, atop the Willis Tower *(p22)*. Those with a head for heights can step into the glass viewing boxes on the 103rd-floor.

**Afternoon**

Hop on the Orange line to State Lake and then cross the river to get to the Magnificent Mile *(p40)*. This small area is most famous for its incredible shopping, with all of the biggest brands found here. Some stores even have restaurants, so stop for lunch in Ralph Lauren at RL *(ralphlauren.com/global-rl-chicago)*. When you're done shopping, finish your trip among the many fun and exciting attractions of Navy Pier *(p34)*. Check out the tasty food offerings here for dinner – Chef Ciccio deli is a great option (be sure to try the Italian roast beef) – and grab a sunset drink at Offshore *(p35)*, the largest rooftop bar in the world.

# 4 DAYS

## Day 1

Kick-start your trip amid the cultural highlights of the Museum Campus. Take your pick from the three top museums: the Field Museum *(p28)*, the Adler Planetarium *(p97)*, or Shedd Aquarium *(p36)*.

> **TRANSPORTATION**
> The route for day one is almost entirely contained within the Loop and the South Loop, so make full use of the "L" train to get around *(p111)*. A trip on the "L" is a requisite part of a visit to Chicago.

Stroll through Grant Park *(p23)*, pausing at the giant Clarence F. Buckingham Memorial Fountain on your way to Mercat a La Planxa *(p101)* for a lunch of colorful tapas. Refueled, continue north to the Art Institute of Chicago *(p24)* for an afternoon of genre-spanning art, including a world-renowned Impressionist collection. Round off the day along the Chicago River, with a stunning 90-minute sunset cruise with the Chicago Architecture Center *(p113)*, taking in the local history and the famed skyscrapers with a knowledgeable guide, before a dinner of local favorites at the Chicago Brewhouse *(chicagobrewhouse.com)*.

**VIEW**
When cycling in Lincoln Park, stop by the Peggy Notebaert Nature Museum *(p89)* to enjoy some of the best views of the park and Chicago's skyline, all to the south.

## Day 2

Today is all about Lincoln Park *(p55)*. If it's a Wednesday or Saturday, grab breakfast at the alfresco Green City Market *(p67)*, then walk 10 minutes to the Chicago History Museum *(p89)*. Step inside to learn about the city's fascinating past from the first people up to the present day. Stroll through the park for a lunch of Chicago favorites at RJ Grunts *(rjgruntschicago.com)*. Then, hop on a Divvy bike *(p113)* at a nearby stop and cycle north, along Alfred Caldwell Lily Pool, to reach the Lakefront Trail on Fullerton Avenue. Cycle down the scenic trail, with views of the city and lake, to North Avenue Beach *(p54)*, where you can relax for a while (if the weather's good). Stick around for dinner at Marge's Still *(margeschicago.com)*, Chicago's oldest pub, and an evening show at the comedy beacon, Second City *(p63)*.

## Day 3

Enjoy a leisurely start today with some retail therapy on the Magnificent Mile *(p40)*. Work your way north along the strip – stopping to check out the Water Tower *(p84)*, one of the few buildings to survive the Great Fire of 1871 – until you reach the John Hancock Center *(p83)*. Head up to the 94th-floor observatory for truly spectacular views from the TILT experience. Return to ground-level and amble over to the Museum of Contemporary Art Chicago *(p83)*. Grab lunch at the on-site restaurant Marisol *(marisol chicago.com)*, then see some of the 2,500 artworks here. Finish the day in Fulton Market, reached via the red and green "L" train from Chicago to Morgan. The area is home to numerous shops, cafes, and galleries, as well as Chicago's top places to eat on "Restaurant Row," the perfect spot for dinner (you can't beat the sushi at Nobu, *p118*).

## Day 4

For your final day, head to the south of Chicago and the Hyde Park area. Devote the morning to the Griffin Museum of Science and Industry *(p30)*. The museum is home to a wide range of exhibits, from space exloration to coal mining, as well as the famous U-505 Submarine. Lunch at nearby Plein Air Cafe *(p107)*, where you can check out Robie House *(p104)* next door, a prime example of Frank Lloyd Wright's Prairie architecture. Burn off your meal with a pleasant walk through Washington Park *(p104)* – you could also visit the DuSable Black History Museum and Education Center *(p105)* while here. Dine on Southern staples at Roux *(roux diner.com)*, before catching a show at the Court Theatre *(p62)*, famous for its reimaginings of classic theater.

**A dinosaur skeleton in the main hall of the Field Museum**

# TOP 10 HIGHLIGHTS



*Attractions at Navy Pier*

NAVY PIER

# EXPLORE THE HIGHLIGHTS

There are some sights in Chicago you simply shouldn't miss, and it's these attractions that make the Top 10. Discover what makes each one a must see on the following pages.

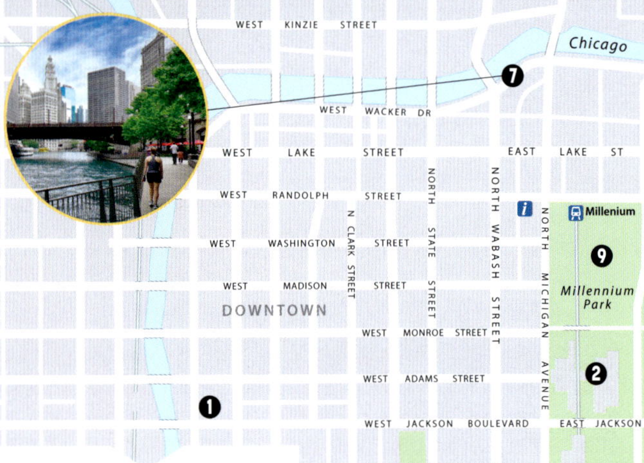


1. Around Willis Tower
2. The Art Institute of Chicago
3. Field Museum
4. Griffin Museum of Science and Industry
5. Navy Pier
6. Shedd Aquarium
7. Chicago Riverwalk
8. The Magnificent Mile
9. Millennium Park
10. Frank Lloyd Wright's Oak Park

AVENUE
STREET
STREET
STREET
AVENUE
NORTH LAKE SHORE DRIVE
Navy Pier Park
Gateway Park
5
River
EAST WACKER DRIVE
Lake Michigan
E RANDOLPH STREET
Monroe Harbor
DRIVE
SOUTH LAKE SHORE DRIVE
6
3
Museum Campus
Greater Chicago
NORTHSIDE
NORTH AVENUE
Oak Park
10
CENTRAL AVENUE
WESTERN AVENUE
EISENHOWER EXPRESSWAY
Area of main map
CICERO
STEVENSON EXPRESSWAY
DAN RYAN EXPWY
FAR SOUTH
0 km 5
0 miles 5
4

# AROUND WILLIS TOWER

J4 233 S. Wacker Dr. Hours vary, check website theskydeck.com

**Although it may no longer be the tallest building in the US, Willis Tower remains the third tallest in the country, and is home to the nation's highest observation deck. For impressive 360-degree city views of sights around the tower, head to the 103rd-floor Skydeck, where those with a head for heights can also step into a series of glass boxes that provide fascinating views of the surrounding sights.**

## 1 John Hancock Center

The Willis Tower's North Side counterpart *(p83)* is this 100-story skyscraper. It houses a retail area, offices, and apartments – as well as an observatory.

## 2 Marina City

Built in 1964, these 65-story buildings *(p48)*, nicknamed the "corncobs," were once the world's tallest residential structures. They now feature a marina and a theater.

## 3 Merchandise Mart

One of the world's largest commercial buildings *(p83)*, by floor area, this 1930s structure was owned by the Kennedy family until the late 1990s.

## 4 United Center

**B5 1901 W. Madison St.**

Known as "the house that Michael built," this vast indoor sports arena and concert venue owes its funding to the fame of the famous basketball player Michael Jordan. It remains the home of the Chicago Bulls, and a statue of Jordan stands proudly outside.

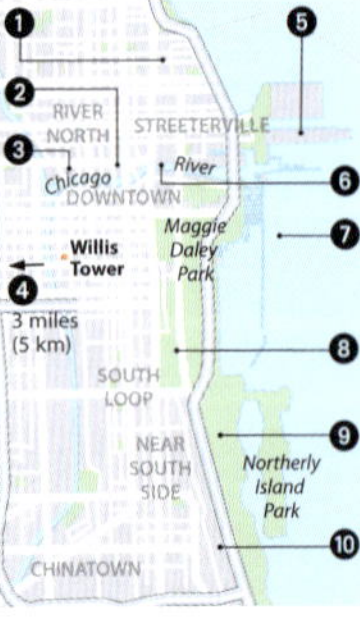


**Glass-enclosed Skydeck on the 103rd floor**

*Clockwise from above* **Soldier Field, the oldest stadium in the NFL; facade of Merchandise Mart; grand Buckingham Fountain in Grant Park**

## 5 Navy Pier

A former naval base turned fun-filled hub *(p34)*, Navy Pier is among Chicago's top attractions.

## 6 Chicago River

The 156-mile- (250-km-) long Chicago River tops world records with its 43 opening bridges. In 1900, an impressive engineering feat resulted in the reversal of the river flow. Every year on St. Patrick's Day the main branch of the river is dyed green.

## 7 Lake Michigan

The third largest of the five Great Lakes, Lake Michigan rarely reaches warm temperatures, even in summer; nevertheless it's a popular swimming spot. On a clear day, you can often see across to the shores of Indiana and Michigan.

## 8 Grant Park

**L6**

Built entirely on a landfill after the Great Chicago Fire *(p9)*, this beautiful park is one of the city's largest and is the venue for music festivals.

## 9 Soldier Field

**L6 425 E. McFetridge Dr.**

Home of the Chicago Bears *(p71)* for over 30 years, this stadium, which opened in 1924, saw the addition of a 63,500-seat structure in 2003.

## 10 McCormick Place

**D5 2301 S. Lake Shore Dr.**

Architect Helmut Jahn designed the present convention center after the original burned down. The complex has four buildings equipped with 40,000 sprinklers.

### TOP 10 TOWER FACTS

1. Willis Tower is 1,450-ft (433-m) high and has 110 stories
2. It weighs a massive 222,500 tons
3. The tower took three years to construct
4. Building costs topped $150 million
5. It contains over 25,000 miles (40,223 km) of electrical cable …
6. … And approximately 43,000 miles (69,200 km) of telephone cable runs through the building
7. Around 20,000 visitors enter and exit each day
8. Over a million people visit the Skydeck annually
9. The elevators travel at an ear-popping 1,600 ft (490 m) per minute
10. Its 16,100 windows are cleaned by machines that are roof-mounted

# THE ART INSTITUTE OF CHICAGO

L4 111 S. Michigan Ave 11am–5pm Wed–Mon (to 8pm Thu)
artic.edu

**Guarded by iconic bronze lions on either side of its stone steps, the Art Institute of Chicago is the Midwest's largest art museum. Housed in a massive Beaux-Arts edifice with a Modern Wing by Renzo Piano, the institute has thousands of artworks from around the globe, and is famous for its Impressionist and Post-Impressionist collections.**

**Edward Hopper's iconic *Nighthawks***

### 1 Nighthawks

One of the most famous images in 20th-century American art, this 1942 painting by Realist Edward Hopper has a melancholy quality. It includes a depiction of fluorescent lighting, new at the time to US cities.

### 2 Nightlife

Archibald John Motley, Jr., associated with the Chicago Black Renaissance movement, was acclaimed for his paintings of African American life in Chicago, including *Nightlife* (1943), which depicts an energetic night in a cabaret.

**EAT**

Enjoy delicious fare at Modern Bar, located in the museum's Modern Wing. It's the perfect spot for a casual lunch with views of the Griffin Court.

### 3 Acrobats at the Cirque Fernando

Children were often the subjects of Pierre-Auguste Renoir's sunny paintings: this luminous 1879 work shows a circus owner's daughters taking a bow after their act.

### 4 Stacks of Wheat Series

From 1890 to 1891, Claude Monet painted 30 views of the haystacks that stood outside his house in France. This museum houses six of these, which illustrate the Impressionist doctrine of capturing the fleeting effects of light in nature.

### 5 At the Moulin Rouge

Unlike many of his fellow Impressionists who painted serene scenes, Henri de Toulouse-Lautrec was drawn to the exuberant nightlife of Paris. This dramatic painting from 1892 celebrates the Moulin Rouge cabaret.

### 6 American Gothic

Grant Wood was inspired by the detailed style of

***American Gothic* by Grant Wood**

Admiring *A Sunday on La Grande Jatte – 1884*

**MUSEUM GUIDE**

Each floor of the museum has a large number of exhibits, which can be subject to change. Generally, the lower level has collections including the Thorne Miniature Room and the Arts of Ancient Egypt, while the first, second and third floors are more focused on painting, from medieval works to the modern day.

the Flemish Renaissance art to create this painting (1930). Though perceived by many as satirical, this artwork celebrates the traditions and culture of the Midwest.

## 7 A Sunday on La Grande Jatte – 1884

Massive and mesmerizing, this painting took French artist Georges Seurat two years to complete. The scene is created from dots of color, based on his study of optical theory, later known as pointillism.

## 8 The Old Guitarist

A young, struggling Pablo Picasso painted this tortured 1903 portrait during his Blue Period. It reflected his grief over a friend's suicide and was a precursor to his own style of Cubism.

## 9 The Child's Bath

The only American artist to have an exhibit in Paris with the Impressionists, Mary Cassatt captures the theme of motherhood in this well-known painting (1893) of a woman bathing a child. Her choice of domestic subjects reflects the limited freedom women experienced at the time.

## 10 America Windows

Unveiled here in 1977, Marc Chagall's stunning stained-glass windows were a gift to the city he loved. The six vibrant panels depict the US as a place of cultural and religious freedom.

**The Art Institute of Chicago Floor Plan**

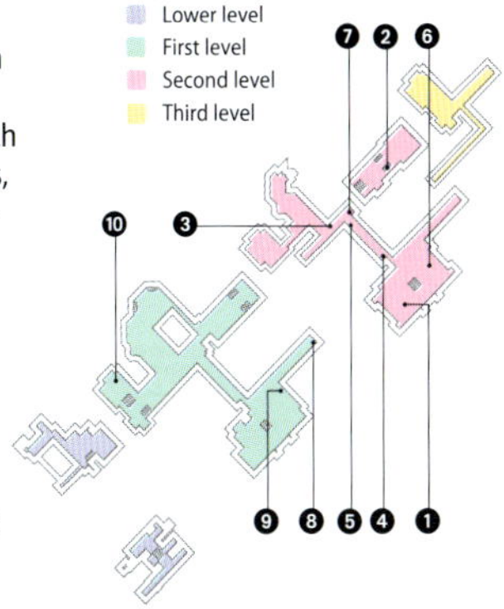

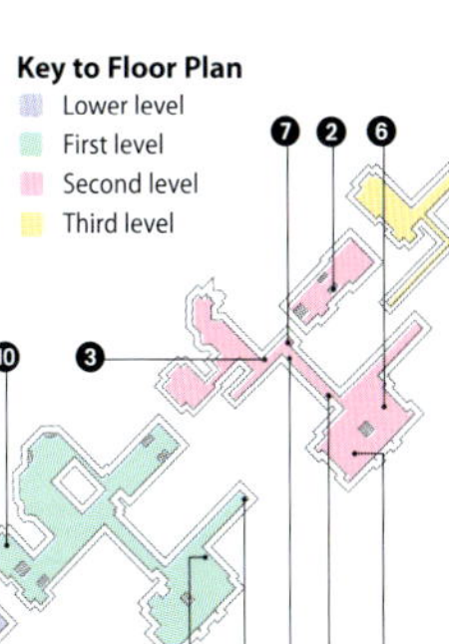

# Collections

### 1. Asian Art

This collection covers 5,000 years and features Japanese screens, Chinese ceramics and jades, and Southeast Asian sculpture. The assemblage of Japanese woodblock prints, such as *Courtesan* (c1. 705–1715) by Kaigetsudo Dohan, is one of the most impressive outside Japan. Look out for the rare early-14th-century scroll painting, *Legends of the Yuzu Nembutsu Sect.*

**European furnishings in one of Thorne's Miniature Rooms**

### 2. The Arts of Africa

Completely reinstalled in 2019, this gallery displays artifacts, sculptures, furniture, masks, jewelry, beadwork, and metalwork from all across the continent. Exhibits are divided into four regions: Northern Africa and the Sahel, Coastal West Africa, Central Africa, and Eastern and Southern Africa. A fifth section focuses exclusively on ceramics and textiles. An audio tour of the gallery is also available.

### 3. European Collection

Arranged chronologically, and spanning the Middle Ages through 1950, this prodigious collection includes a significant array of Renaissance and Baroque art and sculpture. However, its main draw is an extensive collection of nearly 600 Impressionist and Post-Impressionist paintings. Instrumental in its creation was Bertha Honoré Palmer who acquired over 40 Impressionist works (largely ignored in France at the time) for the 1893 World's Columbian Exposition.

### 4. American Arts

This impressive holding contains some 5,500 paintings and sculptures dating from the 1600s to 1950. In addition, paintings and works on paper are on loan from the Terra Foundation collection, and there is a range of decorative arts, including furniture, glass, and ceramics from the 18th century through to the present. A dedicated section, "Arts of the Americas," showcases native art from 5000 BCE to the present.

### 5. Arthur Rubloff Collection of Paperweights

This fabulous collection has over 1,400 paperweights, making it one of the largest of its kind in the world. It displays colorful and exquisite examples from all periods, highlighting different designs and techniques. While most of the pieces originate from 19th-century France, some were also made in America and the United Kingdom.

***Two Sisters (On the Terrace)***
**by Pierre August Renoir**

## 6. Thorne Miniature Rooms

Narcissa Niblack Thorne, a Chicago art patron, combined her love of miniatures with her interest in interiors and decorative arts to create the 68 rooms in this unique Lilliputian installation. Some of the 1 inch:1 foot scale rooms are replicas of specific historic interiors, while others are period recreations.

## 7. Architecture

Chicago's Art Institute houses an architecture and design department, one of only a few in the US. Its collection includes sketches and drawings, which are accessible to the public by appointment. The institute also presents rotating displays featuring architectural pieces, such as a stained-glass window by Frank Lloyd Wright.

## 8. Modern and Contemporary Art

This collection represents the significant art movements in Europe and the US from 1950 to the present day, including Surrealist works by Picasso, Matisse, and Kandinsky, as well as American artists, such as Georgia O'Keeffe.

## 9. Arms and Armor

The Harding Collection of Arms and Armor is one of the largest in America. Over 200 items related to the art of war, including weapons, and complete and partial suits of armor for soldiers – as well as horses are on permanent display. The items showcased originate from Europe, the US, and the Middle East, and date from the 15th through the 19th centuries.

**Art Collections Floor Plan**

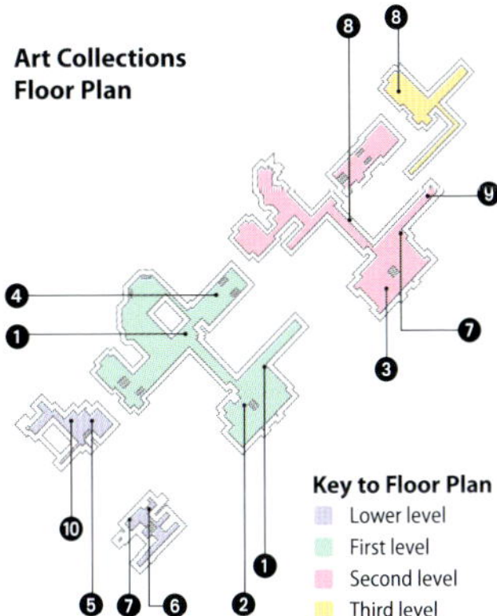


## 10. Photography

Spanning the history of the medium, from its origins in 1839 to the present, this eminent collection was started by Georgia O'Keeffe in 1949 with the donation of works by Alfred Stieglitz. Many modern greats, including Julien Levy, Edward Weston, Paul Strand, and Eugène Atget, are represented here.

**Spears and suits of armor on display**

3

# FIELD MUSEUM

L6 · 1400 S. Lake Shore Dr. · 9am–5pm daily · fieldmuseum.org

**Founded in 1893 to showcase artifacts from the World's Columbian Exposition, the Field Museum was renamed in 1905 in honor of its first major benefactor, Marshall Field. Today, this famous institution offers fascinating insights into natural history and global cultures, both ancient and modern. Its impressive collection includes cultural treasures and rare fossils, alongside a variety of interactive exhibits.**

### MUSEUM GUIDE

The main entrance of the museum is located on the north side, though visitors typically enter from the south, where there is a stop for local buses, trolleys, and cabs. There's a west entrance on the first level, which is suitable for wheelchair access. If you visit on a weekday, be sure to ask the staff about the museum's free Field Favorites tours, which take place daily.

## 1 SUE

This Tyrannosaurus rex, named "SUE" after the archeologist who excavated it, is 13-ft (4-m) high and 42-ft (12.8-m) long. It is also one of the largest and best preserved dinosaur skeletons ever found. Its 600-lb (272-kg) skull is also on display nearby.

## 2 Sobek the Spinosaurus

The third dinosaur in Field's collection, this huge specimen with a crocodile-like head and jaw is the largest predatory dinosaur ever found. The species, found in north Africa, dates back 95 million years.

## 3 Grainger Hall of Gems

This hall features over 600 glittering gems, precious stones, and minerals, all illuminated by fiber-optic lighting. Among the highlights are Tiffany & Co.'s

Browsing the Africa exhibit

stunning Sun God Opal and an Egyptian garnet necklace, which is over 3,400 years old.

## 4 Crown Family PlayLab

This exhibit offers six themed areas, from a science lab to a dinosaur dig, and is full of exciting things for kids to learn.

**SUE, the T. rex, in the main hall**

## 5 Africa

Browse the wares of a Saharan market, see the reality of life for enslaved workers on a ship, and watch a pair of elephants engage in a fight: this exhibit offers an educational journey through African history.

## 6 Inside Ancient Egypt

This part-replica ruin guides visitors through ancient Egyptian bedrooms, tombs, and a typical marketplace.

## 7 Underground Adventure

Enter this "subterranean" ecosystem to wander through a jungle of plant roots and listen to the chatter of a busy ant colony. Note that an extra admission fee is charged here.

## 8 Regenstein Halls of the Pacific

This exibit is a celebration of the Pacific, with local masks and drums, as well as the recorded sounds from the swamps of New Guinea.

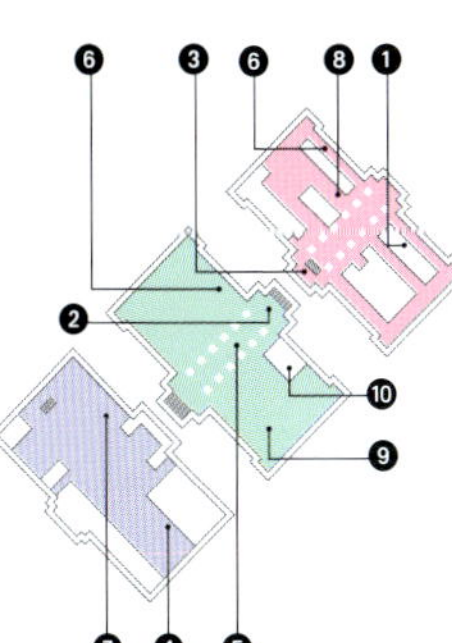


**Key to Floor Plan**
- First level
- Main level
- Upper level

**Field Museum Floor Plan**

## 9 Native Truths: Our Voices, Our Stories

This exhibition tells the stories of Indigenous peoples through their cultural touchstones.

## 10 The Ancient Americas

Explore 13,000 years of human history in the Americas – from Ice Age mammoth hunters to the Aztec Empire and an 800-year-old pueblo – through numerous artifacts, immersive displays, and interactive media.

**Aztec artifact at The Ancient Americas**

# GRIFFIN MUSEUM OF SCIENCE AND INDUSTRY

F6 57th St. and Lakeshore Dr. 9:30am–5:30pm daily (to 4pm Jan–mid-Jun) msichicago.org

**A cultural highlight of the city's South Side, this museum was the first in North America to introduce interactive exhibits. It houses over 800 exhibits, requiring a full day to fully experience, so it's advisable to arrive well rested. Note, tickets can be purchased online in advance and may cost extra on busy weekends.**

### 1 All Aboard the Pioneer Zephyr

Both Art Deco design aficionados and rail buffs are drawn to this streamlined, vintage Zephyr train with its ground-breaking diesel-electric engine.

### 2 Henry Crown Space Center

This, the first manned spacecraft to orbit the moon, offers a peek into the 1960s space race. Photos, space suits, and a training module set the scene, alongside a SpaceX Dragon spacecraft added in 2024.

### 3 Giant Dome Theater

Awe-inspiring science and nature films are shown in this incredible theater, with its five-story wraparound screen. Movies are shown on rotation, with screenings approximately every 50 minutes.

**EAT**
Stan's Donuts *(stansdonuts.com)* and the Museum Kitchen offer light bites, while One Small Snack has takeaway options as well.

### 4 Colleen Moore's Fairy Castle

Star of the silent screen, Colleen Moore commissioned the design of this lavish miniature castle, a study in craft skill, and lovingly filled it with over 2,000 one-twelfth-scaled objects, including the world's smallest Bible.

### 5 U-505 Submarine

Take a tour around this original 1941 German U-boat. The submarine was captured during World War II and is still intact, with an Enigma code-breaking machine.

Beaux Arts-style exterior of the museum

**MUSEUM GUIDE**

The are two main entrances to the museum – the Entry Hall and the Henry Crown Space Center for the Giant Dome Theater. The Entry Hall houses the museum shop, information desk, and Silver Streak train exhibit. Permanent exhibits are displayed throughout the museum.

## 6 The Great Train Story

On this model railroad, over 20 miniature trains race past skyscrapers, across prairies, and over the Rockies to the Pacific Docks – traveling 1,425 ft (437 m) of track that replicates the 2,200-mile (3,540-km) journey from Chicago to Seattle.

## 7 Coal Mine

Venture down a simulated 600 ft (184 m) descent in a traditional shaft elevator to discover how coal was extracted in the 1930s compared to today. The mini train ride enhances the underground illusion.

## 8 Science Storms

This two-story exhibit illustrates basic principles of physics and chemistry using re-creations of natural phenomena, including a 40-ft (12-m) tornado, an enormous Tesla coil that produces lighting, and a 30-ft (9-m) wave tank.

## 9 YOU! The Experience

Discover aspects of the human body and mind from a new perspective. The centerpiece of this exhibit is the massive 13-ft- (4-m-) tall animated 3D human heart, which offers a fascinating interactive experience for visitors of all ages.

**Griffin Museum Floor Plan**

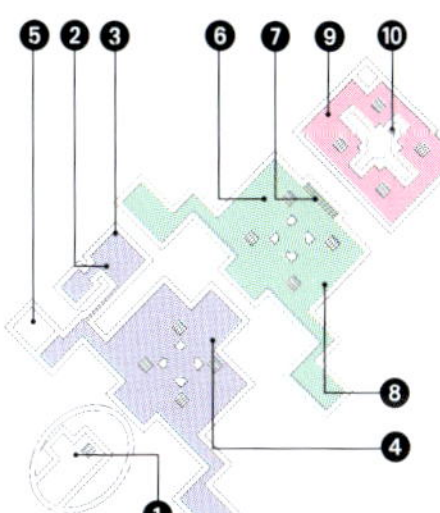


**Key to Floor Plan**

- Lower Level 1
- Main Level 2
- Balcony Level 3

## 10 Take Flight

Explore a fully restored United Airlines *Boeing 727*, with one section preserved as it appeared on its inaugural flight in 1964. Another section reveals its internal electronics and mechanics through a peeled-back exterior.

*Clockwise from right* **Silver Streak train; miniature railroad model, The Great Train Story; *U-505 Submarine* exhibit**

# Exhibits

### 1. Farm Tech
Learn about life on today's farms and the modern technologies that get food from the field to your table. Children can ride in a real combine and take part in a cow-milking challenge.

### 2. Steelmakers
Explore the science of steel, one of earth's most indispensable materials, through hands-on experiences, steel artifacts, and oral histories.

### 3. The Swiss Jolly Ball
The world's largest pinball machine, "Flipper" (also known as the Swiss Jolly Ball), was installed here in 1998. Standing 22-ft- (7-m-) high and 4.5-ft- (15-m-) wide, this impressive machine showcases its complicated mechanics.

### 4. Ships Gallery
Here, model ships chart marine transportation from Egyptian sailboats through to modern ocean liners. Highlights include scale versions of Christopher Columbus's three ships.

### 5. The Art of the Bicycle
This fascinating exhibit explores the pioneering evolution of the bicycle over the last 200 years.

### 6. Yesterday's Main Street
This exhibit recreates a 1910 Chicago cobblestone street, featuring various small shops and a "moving picture" at the Nickelodeon. Visitors can also get a glimpse of the popular fashion trends of the era.

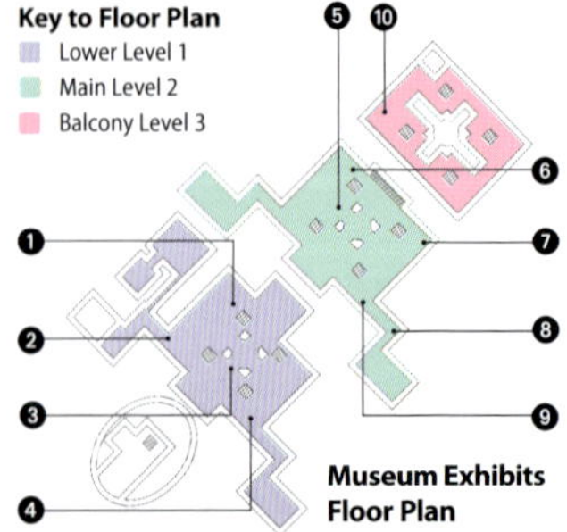

**Museum Exhibits Floor Plan**

**Model aircraft and trains, Transportation Gallery**

### 7. Numbers in Nature: A Mirror Maze
The world of cyberspace comes alive here through educational yet fun hands-on displays.

### 8. The Whispering Gallery
This exhibit has been at the museum since 1938, and still delights passersby. It shows through design how sound waves travel to make the faintest whisper audible at the other end of a room.

### 9. Slime Science
One of the museum's popular Live Science Experiences, this exhibit provides insight into the science of using everyday household items to make sticky-icky slime.

### 10. Transportation Gallery
A full-size *Boeing 727* and a British World War II fighter plane dangle dramatically above a steam locomotive and the world's fastest land vehicle, while visitors explore the forces of flight through computer games.

**TOP 10**
FEATURES OF THE 1893 EXPOSITION

1. First ever Ferris wheel
2. Palace of Fine Arts
3. Midway Plaisance, first separate amusement area at a world's fair
4. Jackson Park, landscaped by designer Frederick Law Olmsted
5. The "Streets of Cairo" exhibit, a re-creation of medieval Cairo
6. Chicago's famous nickname "Windy City," was first introduced
7. A 1,500 lb (680 kg) chocolate *Venus de Milo*
8. A 70-ft- (21-m-) high tower of light bulbs
9. Floodlights used on buildings for the first time
10. 250,000 separate displays on show

## THE MUSEUM'S ORIGINS

**Ferris Wheel, for the 1893 fair**

Built as the Palace of Fine Arts in 1893, the Griffin Museum of Science and Industry is the only building remaining from Daniel H. Burnham's *(p49)* "White City," a name given to the buildings in the fairgrounds due to their distinctive white stucco exterior. It was built for the World's Columbian Exposition, marking the 400th anniversary (albeit one year late) of Christopher Columbus's arrival in the Americas. Burnham, the Director of Works for the World Fair, commissioned architects like Charles Atwood to create structures that would showcase the best in design, culture, and technology. The Field Museum *(p28)* inhabited the building until the 1920s when it moved to its Museum Campus home. Sears Roebuck retail chief Julius Rosenwald then decided that a fortified palace, stripped to its steel frame and rebuilt in limestone, would be the perfect home for a new museum devoted to "industrial enlightenment" and US technological triumphs. The museum opened in 1933 when Chicago hosted its next World's Fair.

**Palace of Fine Arts during the 1893 World's Columbian Exposition**

5

# NAVY PIER

M3 600 E. Grand Ave. 11am–9pm daily (to 10pm Fri & Sat) navypier.org

**A drab slab of concrete in 1995, the Navy Pier has been transformed into a star attraction, drawing millions of visitors annually. Following further renovations in 2018, the People's Energy Welcome Pavilion opened, alongside the stylish Sable at Navy Pier hotel. While entry to the pier is free, most attractions require admission.**

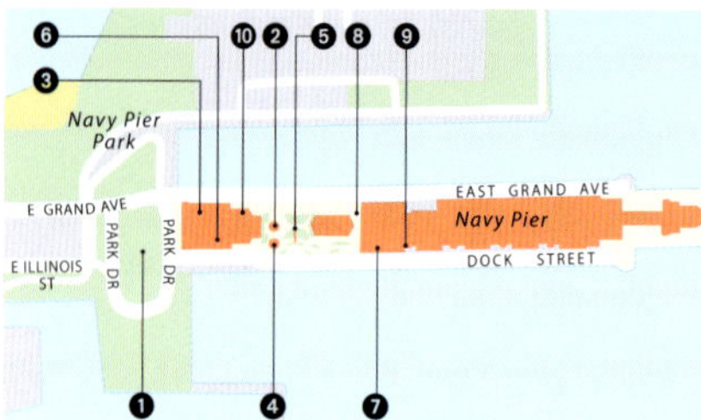


## 3 Flyover

**navypier.org/flyoverchicago**

Opened in 2024, the Flyover offers visitors an exhilarating simulated flight over Chicago, using a massive 65-ft (20-m) video screen and wind effects.

## 1 Polk Bros Park

**10am–8pm Sun–Thu daily (to 10pm Fri & Sat)**

The park in front of Navy Pier features a fountain with 250 jets that mimic the movement of water, schools of fish, or birds. In winter, the park converts into an ice rink.

## 2 Wave Swinger

**10am–9pm Tue–Sun**

Each of the 48 chain-suspended chairs on this thrill ride lifts riders 14 ft (5 m) in the air, and spins until the skyline blurs.

**TOP TIP**

Buy the money-saving Play the Park ticket, which includes all the major attractions.

Musical carousel at the pier

## 4 Musical Carousel

**⏲ 11am–9pm Fri-Sat, 11am–8pm Sun**

A merry-go-round of 36 hand-painted horses and chariots next to the Ferris wheel replicates a similar ride installed at the pier in the 1920s.

## 5 Centennial Wheel

**⏲ 11am–9pm daily (to 10pm Fri & Sat)**

It's hard to miss the pier's popular Ferris wheel. The ride seats eight in each of its 42 enclosed cars. Daytime rides offer fine lake views, while at night, light shows projected onto the wheel create colorful displays.

## 6 Chicago Children's Museum

Kids love this hands-on museum *(p58)* that educates through play. Under-twos get dedicated spaces, including a water room.

## 7 Chicago Shakespeare Theater

This highly respected theater *(p62)* aims to make the Bard accessible to the masses visiting the pier. As well as the Shakespearean classics performed here, productions also include the "Short Shakespeare" for younger audiences.

## 8 Culinary Hub

The pier's dining options include satellite locations of famous Chicago-based spots such as the Billy Goat Tavern *(p87)* and the Original Rainbow Cone *(rainbowcone.com)*.

## 9 Amazing Chicago's Funhouse Maze

**⏲ 11am–8pm daily (to 9pm Fri & Sat)**

This mirror-filled maze leads you on an exciting journey. Expect spinning lights, startling effects, and new perspectives on the city's history.

## 10 Dramatic Fireworks

From Memorial Day to the end of August, an epic fireworks display lights up the sky above the pier every Wednesday at 9pm and Saturday night at 10pm.

**DRINK**

Enjoy drinks, superb views, and live music at the Offshore Rooftop *(offshorerooftop.com)* and the Navy Pier Beer Garden.

Landing point for Navy Pier

6

# SHEDD AQUARIUM

M6 1200 S. DuSable Lake Shore Dr. Hours vary, check website
sheddaquarium.org

**The eponymous John G. Shedd, president of the Marshall Field's department store, donated this Beaux-Arts aquarium to Chicago in 1929. It houses approximately 32,000 marine animals representing 1,500 species, including amphibians, fish, and aquatic mammals. The latter can be seen in the saltwater of the glass-walled Oceanarium.**

**1 Wonder of Water**
This vibrant twin tank exhibit contrasts freshwater and saltwater habitats, with periscopes allowing closer views of over 6,500 fish, 50 species of dense, green undersea plants and coral reef.

**2 Amazon Rising**
This exhibit demonstrates the huge seasonal tides of the world's second-longest river, presenting a year in the Amazon flood plain. It also showcases the rich biodiversity of the Amazon River Basin.

**TOP TIP**

Be sure to visit the underwater viewing galleries, which offer a deep insight into aquatic life.

**Wonder of Water housed in a rotunda**

Classical Greek design of the aquarium

## 5 4-D Experience

This hi-tech theater experience has "special FX seats" that bombard spectators with bubbles, wind, smells, sounds, and other surprises.

## 6 Great Lakes

This exhibit focuses on the diverse marine ecosystems of North America's five Great Lakes. Highlights include a sturgeon touch tank and great displays of alligator snapping turtles, longnose gar, and toothy sea lampreys.

## 7 Oceans

A fascinating exhibit featuring an undersea kelp forest inhabited by leopard sharks, sea dragons, flounders, anemones, moray eel, and octopus, all within caves and rocky reef.

## 8 Animal Chats

Observe sharks close up and learn how they interact with the whole reef community, discover the evolutionary adaptations of sea lions, beluga whales, and dolphins, and investigate the features of penguins.

## 9 Abbott Oceanarium

Underwater galleries afford incredible views of the likes of dolphins and beluga whales swimming through the Oceanarium's vast pools. It is bordered by rocky outcrops and towering pines in a re-creation of the Pacific Northwest coast. Other creatures found in the oceanarium include playful sea otters and California sea lions.

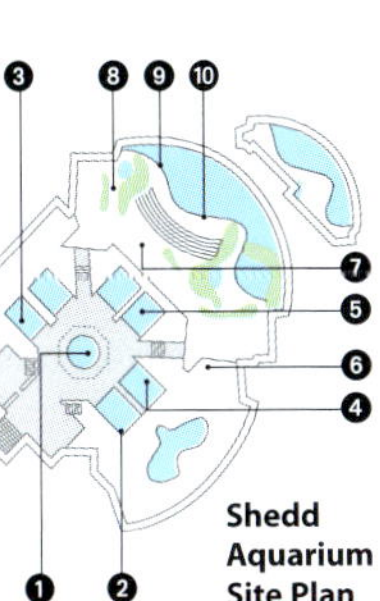


Shedd Aquarium Site Plan

## 10 Polar Play Zone

Located in Shedd's basement is this underwater viewing area is this fun play zone where kids can explore Arctic waters in an interactive miniature submarine. After they're done in the sub, visitors can head to the Icy South viewing deck to watch the Magellanic and rockhopper penguins waddle and swim, and interact with sea stars.

Magellanic penguins at the Polar Play Zone

**EAT**

The aquarium has a number of dining options – Soundings Café serves coffee whille the Bubble Net Food Court offers Chicago dogs and pizzas.

## 3 Virtual Reality

As well as in-person animal encounters, the Shedd offers immersive VR experiences. These live-action journeys allow participants, wearing VR goggles, to swim alongside humpback whales off Antarctica.

## 4 Wild Reef

Gain a daring diver's perspective of whitetip reef, blacktip reef, sandbar, and zebra sharks. The sawfish and fearsome lionfish happily hold their own amid the predator school.

7

# CHICAGO RIVERWALK

M3 chicagoriverwalk.us

**Complementing the gently winding Chicago River for a generous 1.25-mile (2-km) stretch is the Chicago Riverwalk, opened in 2016. Treating walkers to fabulous art, architecture, and recreation, it passes some of the city's most iconic structures. In summer, the area buzzes with people enjoying picnics as kayakers and boat tours drift by, while in winter, visitors bundle up for scenic waterside strolls.**

## 1 River Theater

The main "performance" here is the Chicago River itself. Stretching from Upper Wacker Drive, the open-air auditorium-like seating offers visitors great views of the river, with trees integrated for shady spots.

## 2 Art on the MART

K3 222 W. Merchandise Mart Plaza artonthemart.com

After dark, make your way to the Riverwalk's western end to catch the latest edition of Art on the MART: dazzling public art installations projected onto the Merchandise Mart building. The projections are displayed at dusk.

**TOP TIP**

Kayakers can opt for hourly rentals from Urban Kayaks *(435 E. Chicago Riverwalk).*

## 3 Public Art

From intricate tile mosaics to larger-than-life cast-aluminum flowers, public art of all shapes and sizes adds color and texture to the arcades and plazas along the Riverwalk.

## 4 S. S. Eastland Memorial

The plaque on the LaSalle Street Bridge commemorates the site of the S.S. Eastland disaster, when this ship capsized in 1915, killing 844 people. There's

*Clockwise from below* **Relaxing on the steps, River Theater; al fresco dining beneath DuSable Bridge; Heald Square Monument; Vietnam Veterans Memorial Plaza**

**Cruising along the Chicago Riverwalk**

a moving exhibit in the lobby of Reid Murdoch Center across the bridge.

## 5 McCormick Bridgehouse and Chicago River Museum

99 Chicago Riverwalk
bridgehouse museum.org

The landmark five-story McCormick Bridgehouse is home to an interesting museum tracing the city's relationship with the river and offering insights into Chicago's bridgehouses. It is open for ticketed tours and hosts free lunchtime lectures.

## 6 Vietnam Veterans Memorial Plaza

C5 330 Chicago Riverwalk

In a quiet corner, a set of grassy ledges and a rectangular fountain pay homage to the Vietnam War. A stone wall bears the names of the fallen.

## 7 DuSable Bridge

Built in 1920, this bascule bridge *(p53)* was renamed in 2010 to honor Jean Baptiste Point DuSable, Chicago's first non-native settler *(p8)*. Plaques and sculptures on the bridge commemorate the 1812 Battle of Fort Dearborn.

## 8 Dining Options

Along the water's edge, there are a variety of dining choices, from the full-service experience at City Winery to The Northman's Beer and Cider Garden *(the northman.com)*.

## 9 CAC and Chicago's First Lady Cruises

112 E. Wacker Dr.
firstlady.com/cruises/architecture

A fantastic way to take in the city's skyline is the Chicago's *First Lady* vessel, run by the Chicago Architecture Center (CAC).

## 10 Floating Gardens

The jetty features a series of floating wetlands and water gardens, designed to help grow and preserve the river's natural wildlife habitat.

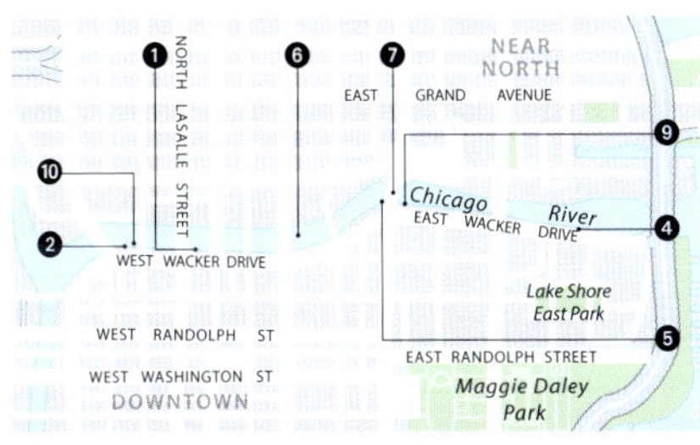

# THE MAGNIFICENT MILE

L2–L3 themagnificentmile.com

**This glitzy strip of stores and striking buildings runs for about a mile (2 km), along North Michigan Avenue. Given the moniker "magnificent," it is popularly known as the Mag Mile. Home to department stores, high-end boutiques, and famous chain stores, this strip is at its best around Christmas when twinkling trimmings provide welcome relief from the often gray days.**

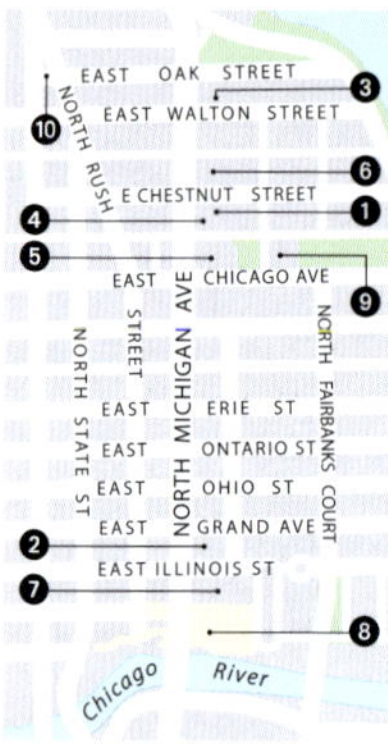

**Skyscrapers on the Magnificent Mile**

## 1 American Girl Place

Eager fans make a beeline for this toy emporium *(p86)*, which stocks varied merchandise from the American Girl doll range. Try the café or visit the salon for the "Styled by You" experience.

**Toy dolls at the American Girl Place**

## 2 InterContinental Chicago Magnificent Mile

This historic hotel *(p119)* exudes 1920s luxury. It was built to serve as a club for the all-male Shrine association. It showcases a range of architectural styles and guests can take a self-guided tour to see the highlights, including the

**EAT**
Choose from a range of fast food in Water Tower Place. Cold Moon Cafe *(coldmooncafe.us)* and JoJo's Shake Bar *(jojosshakebar.com)* are worth a try.

Enjoying the TILT at the John Hancock Center

stunning swimming pool on its 14th floor.

## 3 The Drake Hotel

This elegant hotel *(p52)* became an instant glamor hotspot when it opened on New Year's Eve in 1920. Marilyn Monroe was among the stars who visited. High tea here is a treat.

## 4 Water Tower Place

**835 N. Michigan Ave.**
**11am–7pm Mon–Thu, 11am–8pm Fri & Sat, noon–6pm Sun**
**shopwatertower.com**

Housing a busy shopping mall, this complex is one of the world's tallest reinforced concrete buildings. Its 70-plus shops include a branch of the LEGO® Store and a Broadway-style theater.

## 5 Chicago Water Works and Pumping Station

Dwarfed by the surrounding skyscrapers, this structure *(p84)* is among the few that survived the Great Fire of 1871. The water tower, designed by William W. Boyington, was completed in 1869, while the pumping station still functions today.

## 6 John Hancock Center

Built in 1969, this 100-story skyscraper *(p83)*, officially known as 875 North Michigan Avenue, was once the world's second-tallest building. Visitors can enjoy exhilarating views of Chicago from the 94th-floor observatory and the thrilling TILT viewing experience.

## 7 Tribune Tower

The result of a design contest organized by the *Chicago Tribune* newspaper *(p84)*, this Gothic tower is both adored and abhorred by locals. Either way, it's a dramatic Mag Mile landmark.

## 8 Pioneer Court

This sprawling plaza near Tribune Tower often hosts public art exhibits. Several boat and river cruise operators set up kiosks here – ideal for booking in advance and same-day tours.

## 9 Museum of Contemporary Art Chicago

Off Michigan Avenue, the strip's cultural gem, this museum *(p83)* features compelling temporary exhibits, a sculpture garden, and performing arts.

## 10 Oak Street

Oak Street *(p66)* is a premium retail space lined with high-end stores, and marks one end of the Mag Mile.

Chicago Water Works and Pumping Station

9

# MILLENNIUM PARK

L4 · 201 E. Randolph St. · 312-742-1168 · 6am–11pm daily

**Designed to celebrate the turn of the 21st century with the reclamation of a former railroad yard in an industrial corner of Grant Park, Millennium Park exceeded its goals in becoming a civic magnet. Art, architecture, the performing arts, and nature each play a role in the popular park, which hosts free summer concerts and special events, and draws visitors year-round to its perennial attractions.**

**1 Crown Fountain**
Designed by Spanish artist Jaume Plensa, the Crown Fountain features two 50-ft- (15-m-) high glass-block towers that broadcast the videotaped faces of Chicago residents – keep watching to see if they blink. In summer it's a popular splash park.

**2 Cloud Gate Sculpture**
Designed by sculptor Anish Kapoor, the work *Cloud Gate* resembles an enlarged, reflective kidney bean, prompting its nickname, "The Bean." A selfie taken here in front of the work reflects the surrounding skyline and is Chicago's signature souvenir.

**3 Lurie Garden**
The 15-ft- (5-m-) high "shoulder" hedges edging the Lurie Garden pay homage to the "City of Big Shoulders" cited by Carl Sandburg in his poem *Chicago*. They shelter a delicate perennial garden spanned by a hardwood footbridge crossing shallow water.

**Crowds strolling in Lurie Garden**

**4 Jay Pritzker Pavilion**
Designed by the architect Frank Gehry, the centerpiece performing arts venue of the park is framed in flying wings of steel. A criss-crossing trellis

The Gehry-designed Jay Pritzker Pavilion

of speaker-supporting steel pipes extends out over the lawn of this huge concert venue.

## 5 BP Bridge

The BP bridge, connecting Millennium Park to neighboring Maggie Daley Park *(p79)*, was also designed by Frank Gehry. The steel-clad winding structure offers views of Lake Michigan, the skyline, and Millennium Park, and takes an intentionally indirect route.

## 6 Ice-Skating Rink

The Millennium Park ice-skating rink, which is generally open between December and March (weather permitting), is free. This perhaps accounts for the throngs of skaters here, eager to glide under "The Bean."

## 7 Harris Theater

Located in the northern fringe of the park, the Harris Theater is a reputable platform for music and dance; some 35 Chicago performing arts companies call the Harris home, including Hubbard Street Dance, Music of the Baroque, and Chicago Opera Theater.

## 8 Nichols Bridgeway

Architect Renzo Piano, who designed the Modern Wing addition to the Art Institute of Chicago, worked on this bridge, which slowly rises from the park to the third story of the museum across the street.

## 9 Millennium Hall

The only restaurant in the park, Millennium Hall has one of the city's biggest beer gardens. The food served here includes a mix of casual burgers and upscale fare, which is the perfect accompaniment to the views of the city skyline. In warm weather, tables sprawl out onto the terrace, which serves as the skating rink in winter.

**TOP TIP**

Get the best views of the park and the city skyline from the peak of BP Bridge.

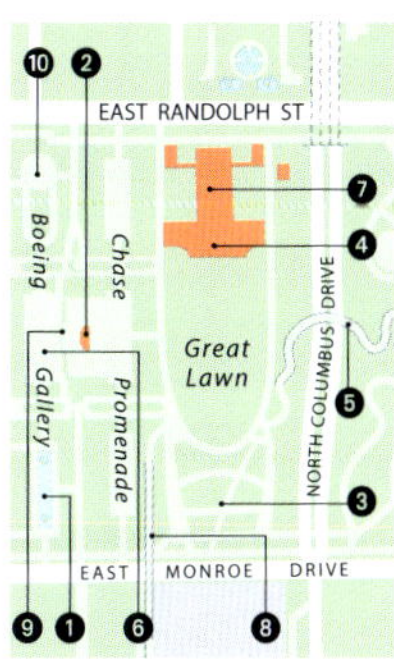


## 10 Millennium Monument

At the park's northwest corner at Wrigley Square is this semicircular peristyle. Its row of 40-ft (12-m) Doric-style columns brings to mind the original classical monument that stood here in the first half of the 20th century. It's now an attractive backdrop to the modern city.

**Doric-style columns of the Millenium Monument**

# FRANK LLOYD WRIGHT'S OAK PARK

A4 1010 Lake St. flwright.org/tour/home-and-studio

**A charming suburb, 7 miles (11 km) west of downtown Chicago, Oak Park houses the world's largest collection of Frank Lloyd Wright-designed buildings. It was here that Wright developed his distinctive Prairie style, a radical departure from the typical styles of the era. A stroll through the park's tree-lined streets reveals how Wright's architecture stands apart from the norm.**

**Church sanctuary at Unity Temple**

## 1 Beachy House

238 Forest Ave.

This impressive 1906 home contradicts many of Wright's trademarks. Instead of just stucco and wood, or brick and concrete, he used them all: it also has a seven-gabled, rather than a hipped, roof.

## 2 Arthur Heurtley House

318 Forest Ave.

Wright's beautiful 1902 house is absolute Prairie, with its low, wide chimney, and band of art-glass windows that makes the overhanging roof appear to float.

## 3 Pleasant Home

217 South Home Ave.

A 30-room Prairie-style 1897 home built by George Maher, Pleasant Home was the first in Oak Park to have electricity. This architectural gem holds a compact history museum, with exhibits relating to Edgar Rice Burroughs, a former local resident and creator of Tarzan.

## 4 Nathan Moore House

333 Forest Ave.

Out of financial desperation, Wright built this charming Tudor-style home for his neighbor, Nathan Moore. After a fire destroyed its top floors in 1922, Wright's modifications echoed his West Coast concrete block houses.

## 5 Unity Temple

875 West Lake St.

Designed in 1908 to serve Oak Park's Unitarian Universalist Congregation, this compact church superbly demonstrates Wright's varied use of poured concrete, here for both structural and decorative purposes.

## 6 Edwin Cheney House

520 North East Ave.

The Edwin Cheney House sparked a tragic love affair between Wright and Mamah Cheney, leading him to abandon his family and practice. Mamah and her children were murdered at Wright's home by a servant in 1914.

**EAT**

For amazing pastries, stop by Broken Tart *(broken tart.com)* at 1108 Chicago Ave., which is a short walk from the Frank Lloyd Wright Home and Studio.

## 7 The Bootleg Houses

1019/1027/1031 Chicago Ave.

Wright lost his job over these three private commissions, built while he was employed by Louis H. Sullivan *(p49)*. Though Queen Anne-like in style, they hint at the design elements that were to be his hallmarks.

## 8 Frank Lloyd Wright Home and Studio

951 Chicago Ave.

312-994-4000

10am–4pm daily

Built in 1889 when the famous architect moved to Oak Park, this is the house where Wright designed over 150 structures. Its children's playroom is luminous with his signature art-glass windows.

## 9 Charles Matthews House

432 North Kenilworth Ave.

Chicago architects Thomas Eddy Tallmadge and Vernon S. Watson designed this magnificent 1909 Prairie-style residence for a wealthy pharmacist. Among the remarkable interior details are the Prairie-inspired light fixtures and folding art-glass doors.

## 10 Harry Adams House

710 Augusta Blvd.

This striking 1913 home marks the last of Wright's Oak Park houses and features several of the elements that made him famous, such as exquisite stained glass and a low overhanging roof. It is also the only building in Oak Park to have the unique addition of a car port, which was considered to be more economical than a traditional garage.

**FRANK LLOYD WRIGHT**

After moving to Oak Park in 1889, Wright (1867–1959) pioneered a new vision for American architecture: the Prairie style. More than a third of his life's work was done at his Oak Park studio. Though his personal life was wrought with scandal, he established himself as the first celebrity architect of global renown.

**Frank Lloyd Wright Home and Studio**

# TOP 10 OF EVERYTHING



*Spiral staircase at The Rookery*

# SKYSCRAPERS

**Spectacular light court, The Rookery**

## 1 The Rookery

One of the earliest skyscrapers, this 1888 landmark *(p76)* combines traditional wall-bearing and steel-frame construction. The latter made it possible for its architects, Burnham and Root, to design an open interior, with offices set around a central light well.

## 2 John Hancock Center

The tapering, 100-story John Hancock Center *(p83)* is somewhat overshadowed by the taller Willis Tower but is arguably more distinctive. Created by Skidmore, Owings & Merrill, who also designed the Willis, it features its own observatory on the 94th floor.

## 3 Auditorium Theater

L5 50 E. Ida B. Wells Dr.
312-341-2389

Built by architectural firm Adler and Sullivan in 1889, the ornate Auditorium originally housed a hotel and offices, and featured one of the first public air-conditioning systems. Its revamped theater has near-perfect acoustics.

## 4 Reliance Building

The steel frame of this 1895-built skyscraper *(p78)* allowed for its glass facade. It offers a fine example of the Chicago window, characterized by a bay window flanked by two narrow, double-hung windows. Now occupied by the Staypineapple *(staypineapple.com)* hotel, its interior preserves original features.

## 5 860–880 Lake Shore Drive Apartments

L2

Built in 1949–51, these two high-rise apartment buildings are Chicago landmarks and were added to the National Register of Historic Places in 1980. Architect Mies van der Rohe perfected the "less is more" approach, which many others later copied.

## 6 Willis Tower

This soaring tower *(p22)*, built in 1973 for retailer Sears Roebuck and Co. (who have since moved out), can be seen from almost anywhere in the city. Its Skydeck affords sensational views.

## 7 Aqua Tower

L3 225 N. Columbus Dr.

The exterior of the 82-story Aqua Tower appears to undulate due to the varying elevations of its balconies. Architect Jeanne Gang cites the striated limestone outcroppings common in the Great Lakes region as the inspiration for this effect.

## 8 Monadnock Building

Constructed in two stages, this Loop edifice *(p78)* represents the evolution of skyscraper architecture. The northern half was built in 1891 using solely wall-bearing construction, while the southern half was built two years later and used the then-emerging steel-frame technology still used today.

## 9 Tribune Tower

Built in 1925, this Neo-Gothic building *(p84)*, with a cathedral-like

**Marina City's twin towers on the banks of the Chicago River**

buttress atop it, was the former headquarters of the Chicago Tribune. Its facade contains stones from 120 global landmarks, including China's Great Wall.

## 10 Marina City

K4 300 N. State St.

Designed by Bertrand Goldberg Associates and constructed between 1959 and 1964, Marina City is an iconic complex on the edge of the Chicago River. Its twin cylindrical towers – often likened to giant corncobs – pay symbolic tribute to the Midwest's agricultural heritage. Conceived as a "city within a city," the complex includes residential apartments, offices, retail spaces, a marina, a theater, parking garages, and even a bowling alley. While the apartments offer spectacular views of the city and river, their distinctive round shape creates some unique interior decorating challenges.

## TOP 10 CHICAGO ARCHITECTS

**Frank Lloyd Wright**

**1. William Le Baron Jenney (1832–1907)**
The "Father of the skyscraper," Jenny designed the first all-metal-framed structure, the Home Insurance Building.

**2. Daniel H. Burnham (1846–1912)**
Visionary city planner and architect, Burnham created White City *(p33)*.

**3. Louis H. Sullivan (1856–1924)**
The creator of the "form follows function" doctrine designed buildings based on their intended use.

**4. Frank Lloyd Wright (1867–1959)**
Inspired by the wide open spaces of the Midwest, Wright *(p45)* was the originator of the Prairie style.

**5. Marion M. Griffin (1871–1961)**
In 1895, Griffin was hired by Frank Lloyd Wright to help pioneer Prairie-style architecture.

**6. Ludwig Mies van der Rohe (1886–1969)**
A minimalist architect, Mies pioneered the modern glass-and-steel box.

**7. Bertrand Goldberg (1913–1997)**
Designer of Marina City, Goldberg is noted for his curvilinear shapes.

**8. Beverly L. Green (1915–1957)**
Illinois' first female African American architect, Green helped design the UNESCO headquarters in Paris.

**9. Gertrude L. Kerbis (1926–2016)**
Kerbis designed the Rotunda at O'Hare Airport and the Skokie Public Library in Chicago's suburbs.

**10. Jeanne Gang (b. 1964)**
Designer of the award-winning Aqua Tower, Gang is a contemporary innovator among skyscraper designers.

# SPECIALIST MUSEUMS

## 1 Swedish American Museum

B3 5211 N. Clark St. 10am–4pm Tue–Fri, 11am–4pm Sat & Sun swedishamericanmuseum.org

Located in Andersonville, a historic neighborhood settled by Scandinavian immigrants, this tiny museum features a collection of personal items brought over by early settlers, supplemented by temporary exhibitions on Swedish culture. The museum includes the adjacent Brunk Children's Museum of Immigration, which traces the journey of Swedish immigrants to the United States, made in the 19th century.

## 2 National Hellenic Museum

H5 333 S. Halsted St. 10am–4pm Thu–Sun nationalhellenicmuseum.org

Situated in the city's Greektown, this museum is dedicated to celebrating Hellenic culture and the Greek immigrant experience in America.

## 3 DuSable Black History Museum and Education Center

Named for Jean Baptiste Point duSable, Chicago's first non-Indigenous settler (who was also of African descent), this enthralling museum *(p105)* chronicles the Black experience in the US. It features a powerful exhibit on slavery, complete with shackles, while displays cover topics such as African hair art and the *Kwanzaa* holiday celebration.

## 4 Jane Addams Hull-House

Nobel Peace Prize-winning social reformer Jane Addams set up a settlement house in this Victorian mansion *(p99)* in 1889 to provide social services to Chicago's immigrant population. In addition to her original art and furniture, the house stages temporary exhibits related to the social settlement that provided day care, counseling, and education to the working class.

## 5 National Veterans Art Museum

B4 4041 N. Milwaukee Ave. 10am–4pm Tue–Sat nvam.org

This small yet fascinating museum showcases artwork by hundreds of veterans, inspired by combat and military service, in its permanent and rotating exhibitions. The museum houses over 1,500 works of art, and also manages a community arts project, providing a space for local artists to express their perspectives on war.

Day of the Dead display at the Museum of Mexican Art

## 6 Ukrainian Institute of Modern Art

B4 2320 W. Chicago Ave. Noon–4pm Wed–Sun uima-chicago.org

This tiny institute in the colorful Ukrainian Village neighborhood features rotating cultural programs, exhibitions, literary events, film screenings, and concerts. Its permanent collection includes works by Chicago artists, as well as by painters and sculptors of Ukrainian descent.

## 7 National Museum of Mexican Art

B5 1852 W. 19th St. 10am–5pm Tue–Sun nationalmuseumofmexicanart.org

The largest Latino museum in the US explores the culture *sin fronteras* (without boundaries), showcasing works from Mexican and Mexican-American communities. Highlights of the collection include pre-colonial ceramics, Day of the Dead candelabras, and prints by Diego Rivera.

## 8 Institute for the Study of Ancient Cultures

Founded in 1919, this museum *(p103)* at the University of Chicago showcases the work of the university's researchers and houses fantastic historical objects found during excavations in Egypt, Mesopotamia, Nubia, Persia, Syria, Anatolia, and ancient Megiddo. It also hosts regular temporary exhibitions.

## 9 Block Museum of Art

B2 40 Arts Circle Dr., Evanston Noon–8pm Wed–Fri, noon–5pm Sat & Sun blockmuseum.northwestern.ed

Housed in a glass-and-limestone building designed by local architect Dirk Lohan, this museum features a collection of paintings, drawings, and sculpture. It also offers rotating exhibitions, lectures, and workshops.

## 10 International Museum of Surgical Science

F4 1524 N. Lake Shore Dr. 9:30am–5pm Mon–Fri, 10am–5pm Sat & Sun imss.org

Opened in 1954, this museum houses 5,000 rare medical texts. Murals and sculptures pay tribute to the medical profession, while ancient Peruvian skulls hints at early surgical attempts.

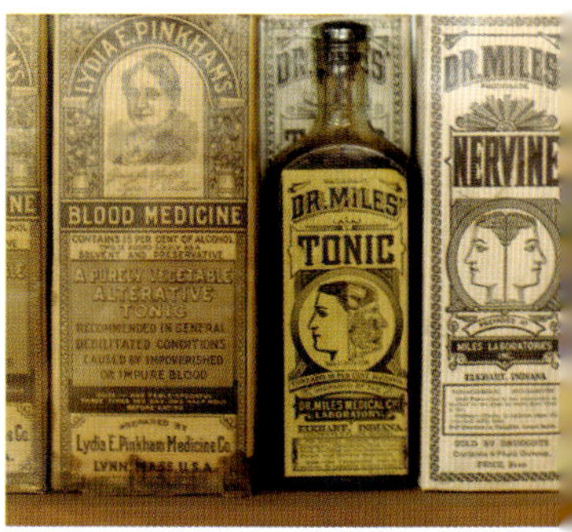

Antique medical tonics, Museum of Surgical Science

# MOVIE LOCATIONS

**Andy Garcia in a scene from *Hero* at the Drake**

## 1 Drake Hotel

L2 140 East Walton Place
thedrakehotel.com

In the film *Hero* (1992), John Bubber (Andy Garcia) deceives the public into believing he's a hero. Wracked with guilt, he resolves to jump from a window at The Drake. Filming was interrupted when hotel guests arrived, prompting director Stephen Frears to protest, nearly resulting in his arrest.

## 2 Willis Tower

Director Christopher Nolan filmed much of his acclaimed superhero movie *The Dark Knight* (2008) around Chicago. In one scene, when Batman is atop the landmark Willis Tower *(p22)*, Christian Bale (who played the superhero) actually stands on the edge of the building instead of a stunt man.

## 3 Daley Center and Plaza

Daley Plaza *(p79)* was the setting for a chase scene in the classic movie *The Blues Brothers* (1980). Stars John Belushi and Dan Aykroyd, playing ex-criminal brothers, crash a car through the center's plate-glass windows, specially installed for the filming.

## 4 DuSable Bridge

In *Chain Reaction* (1996), Keanu Reeves is a student at the University of Chicago *(p102)* who is framed for murder. In a nail-biting chase scene, he tries to escape by running up the DuSable Bridge as it's raised.

## 5 Palmer House Hilton

K4 17 E Monroe St
hilton.com

Wrongly accused and convicted of murder, Dr. Richard Kimble (Harrison Ford) dodges the authorities led by

**Willis Tower as seen in *The Dark Knight***

Tommy Lee Jones to prove his innocence in *The Fugitive*. He winds up in a pulse-pounding chase through this grand hotel onto its roof, down its elevator shaft, and into the hotel's laundry room.

## 6 Marina City

This architectural landmark *(p22)* has appeared in numerous Hollywood movies over the decades. The Steve McQueen-fronted thriller *The Hunter* (1979) shot a memorable chase scene here: a stunt car drove straight off the building and into the river below. The complex can also be seen in the 2021 slasher film *Candyman*.

## 7 The Art Institute of Chicago

The high-school comedy *Ferris Bueller's Day Off* (1986) stars Matthew Broderick as a student, who skips school and spends an action-packed day in Chicago with his girlfriend (Mia Sara) and best friend (Alan Ruck). Their day includes a visit to the Art Institute of Chicago *(p24)*, where Broderick and Sara share a kiss in front of a Chagall-designed window, while Ruck stares intensely at *A Sunday on La Grande Jatte – 1884*.

## 8 Wrigley Field

The 1914-vintage Wrigley Field *(p89)*, home to the Chicago Cubs, has starred in numerous baseball movies, including *The Natural* (1984), *A League of Their Own* (1992), and *Rookie of the Year* (1993). It also has a cameo in *The Blues Brothers* and *Ferris Bueller's Day Off*.

## 9 Victory Gardens Biograph Theater

**L4** **2433 N. Lincoln Ave.**
**victorygardens.org**

Opened in 1914, this historic Lincoln Park theater is famous as the site where bank robber John Dillinger was shot and killed by FBI agents in 1934 – this scene was later recreated and filmed here for the Johnny Depp movie *Public Enemies* (2009). The theater also appears briefly in *High Fidelity* (2000).

## 10 Union Station

**J4** **210 S. Canal St.**

Union Station was featured in *The Untouchables* (1987). Starring Robert DeNiro as the famous gangster Al Capone and Kevin Costner as Elliot Ness, the movie is based on a true story. In an unforgettable shoot-out scene, a baby carriage falls in slow motion down the stairs and is saved at the last moment by Ness's partner.

**Union Station staircase featuring in *The Untouchables***

# PARKS AND BEACHES

## 1 North Avenue Beach

Chicago's most popular, family-friendly beach, North Avenue *(p90)* attracts plenty of of city dwellers in the summer. Its striking ocean-liner shaped bathhouse includes shower rooms, umbrella rentals, snack vendors, and a rooftop restaurant. Beach volleyball courts and a seasonal outdoor gym are a big draw.

## 2 Oak Street Beach

L1

At the edge of the chic Gold Coast, Oak Street Beach reflects the elegance of its environs. Its crescent-shaped shoreline is often filled with sunbathers and is the closest beach to the Magnificent Mile *(p40)*, making it a perfect spot to dip your toes after a shopping spree.

## 3 Montrose Beach

C3

Montrose Beach, the city's largest public beach, is especially popular with families. Ideal for swimming, it has a changing house and shower facilities. Visitors can also play volleyball, try sailing, and enjoy a network of trails for running and biking. At its southeastern end is the Montrose Beach Dunes Natural Area, once a landfill, now restored to include rare habitats that attract over 300 bird species, including the endangered Great Lakes piping plover. Kayak rentals are also available here in summer.

## 4 Millennium and Grant Parks

Besides being a center for world-class art, music, architecture, and landscape design, Millennium Park *(p42)* offers winter ice-skating, interactive public art, al fresco dining, and classical music concerts and film screenings. Together with the adjoining Grant Park, which hosts many festivals, it constitutes one of the finest, user-friendly green spaces in Chicago.

## 5 Maggie Daley Park

Named after Chicago's former first lady, this park *(p79)* lies directly east of Millennium Park. It offers a wide range of attractions, including a seasonal ice-skating ribbon, climbing walls, and an elaborate playground for children. There are also tennis courts, picnic tables, and a garden dedicated to cancer survivors.

## 6 Jackson Park

F6

Originally laid out by famed landscape designer Frederick Law Olmsted for the 1893 World's Columbian Exposition, Jackson Park – along with the Griffin

Skyscrapers towering over North Avenue Beach

Museum of Science and Industry (*p30*) – is among the few developments still remaining from that historic World's Fair. This South Side park includes a Japanese garden with colorful lanterns, and a bird sanctuary on an island in a peaceful lagoon. It is also the site of the forthcoming Barack Obama Presidential Center.

**Relaxing in the garden at the Lincoln Park Conservatory**

## 7 Lincoln Park
F3

The greenway of Lincoln Park extends from North Avenue to Hollywood Avenue, forming a recreational stretch between the lakefront and nearby neighborhoods. In Chicago's early days, the park's southern section served as a cemetery for Civil War victims, who were later exhumed and interred elsewhere to make way for the park. Today, Lincoln Park is the North Side's counterpart to Grant Park, offering many attractions – including the Lincoln Park Zoo (*p90*), the Peggy Notebaert Nature Museum (*p89*), and the Lincoln Park Conservatory (*p90*) – alongside beaches, harbors, and bike paths.

## 8 Washington Square
K2

Located opposite the historic Newberry Library, Washington Square is a peaceful spot for resting and admiring the handsome 1892 building. Its many benches make it a popular lunchtime retreat for picnicking office workers.

## 9 Northerly Island

A peninsula jutting out into Lake Michigan south of the Alder Planetarium, Northerly Island (*p98*) is home to prairie plants, walking trails, and fountains. It also hosts concerts and special events at an outdoor stage that can seat up to 30,000 people on its lawn.

## 10 Ping Tom Memorial Park
K6

Named in honor of a noted Chinese civic leader, this green space features Chinese design elements. Its field house includes a swimming pool, and in summer, the boathouse offers kayak rentals.

# OFF THE BEATEN PATH

## 1 University of Chicago

Funded by oil magnate John D. Rockefeller, this university *(p103)* opened in 1892. Its campus is home to an attractive Neo-Gothic quad, the Institute for the Study of Ancient Cultures *(p103)*, the Smart Museum of Art, the soaring Rockefeller Memorial Chapel, and the Robie House *(p104)*.

## 2 Chicago Botanic Garden

**A1 1000 Lake Cook Rd., Glencoe 10am–8pm daily chicagobotanic.org**

North of Evanston lies this lovely set of landscaped gardens, which hosts a number of shows and special events throughout the year. The most popular are the Rose Garden, the Japanese Garden, and the charming English Walled Garden.

## 3 Baha'i Temple

**A1 100 Linden Ave., Wilmette 6am–6pm daily bahai.us**

This exquisite white structure is one of only eight Baha'i temples in the world. Its nine entrance doors symbolize the many paths through which people can seek God. After sunset, spotlights illuminate its intricate design, highlighting its ethereal beauty.

**Filigreed dome of the Baha'i Temple**

## 4 Evanston

**B2 enjoyevanston.com**

This lively suburb is home to a mix of restaurants, galleries, and shops. Notable attractions include Northwestern University's Block Museum of Art *(p51)* and the historic Grosse Point Lighthouse *(grossepointlighthouse.net)*.

## 5 Brookfield Zoo

**A6 8400 W. 31st St., Brookfield 331 9:30am–6pm daily brookfieldzoo.org**

Home to over 3,400 animals, this popular zoo features themed, naturalistic environments that reflect diverse wildlife habitats. Explore zones like Tropic World, where simulated thunderstorms occur regularly, and Habitat Africa!, whose Forest exhibit houses the elusive okapi. The Rainforest Aviary Feeding Adventure lets visitors feed birds with help from zoo experts.

## 6 Bronzeville

**C5**

A bronze memorial at Martin Luther King Jr. Drive and 35th Street honors the journey many African Americans made to this neighborhood as they fled oppression in the South during the early 20th century. Nearby, sidewalk plaques pay tribute to local luminaries. Often called Chicago's answer to Harlem, Bronzeville offers jazz and blues clubs, graceful mansions, and some of city's finest soul food.

## 7 Hemingway Birthplace

**A5 339 N. Oak Park Ave, Oak Park 10am–5pm Sat, 1–5pm Thu–Fri & Sun Dec–mid-Mar: Sun hemingwaybirthplace.com**

Award-winning novelist Ernest Hemingway was born in suburban

Oak Park *(p44)* in 1899. This beautifully preserved 1890 Queen Anne-style townhouse where he was born and lived until the age of six is open for engaging guided tours.

## 8 Pullman National Historical Park

**B6 610 E. 111th St. 10am–4pm Wed–Sun (from 9am mid-Dec–mid-Mar) nps.gov/pull**

Named a National Historical Park in 2022, this industrial town was conceived in the 1880s by railroad magnate George Pullman. The planned utopia had apartments, shops, and a hospital, but failed after a strike in 1894, when a wage cut made rents unaffordable.

## 9 Illinois Institute of Technology (IIT)

**C5 10 W. 35th St. iit.edu**

In 1940, Ludwig Mies van der Rohe planned the campus of this university. He also designed more than 20 of the buildings, which demonstrate his design philosophies. On arrival, stop by the on-campus visitor center for information and docent- or iPod-guided tours.

## 10 Garfield Park Conservatory

**B5 300 N. Central Park Ave. 10am–5pm daily (to 8pm Wed) garfieldconservatory.org**

Established between 1906 and 1907, Garfield Park Conservatory is one of the largest greenhouse conservatories in the US. Landscape architect Jens Jensen envisioned a natural landscape under glass, a vision brought to life with the help of architects Schmidt, Garden, and Martin. Beneath glass-domed roofs, flora from around the world thrives in greenhouses. Information panels guide visitors through six distinct areas, including a Children's Garden and the Sweet House, which features tropical crops like cacao and sugarcane. Two grand exhibition halls host special events through the year.

**Exhibition on the 1894 strike, Pullman National Historical Park**

# FAMILY ATTRACTIONS

**Rock climbing at Maggie Daley Park**

## 1 Maggie Daley Park

This 20-acre (8-ha) park *(p79)*, tucked between Millennium Park and Lake Shore Drive, is a superb recreation area. Its vast Play Garden has a pirate ship, swinging bridge, rope ladder, and an Enchanted Forest with meandering paths and a rolling Wave Lawn. A seasonal ice ribbon makes a curvy path around the park's two rock climbing walls, which include routes for beginners as well as for advanced climbers. Note that for rock climbing, children must be able to properly fit into the harnesses provided, which usually do not fit those under the age of four.

## 2 Lincoln Park Conservatory

Located in the heart of Lincoln Park's expansive swathe of green, this beautiful conservatory *(p90)* is a haven of climate-controlled greenhouses, namely The Palm House, Orchid House, Fern Room, and Show House, all containing plant species from around the world to make up an urban jungle of sorts. It offers the perfect kid-friendly escape from the elements.

## 3 Chicago Children's Museum

M3 700 E. Grand Ave. 10am–5pm daily chicagochildrensmuseum.org

The engrossing, imaginative exhibits at this museum emphasize hands-on learning – be it digging up a dinosaur bone or designing a water channel. A central, three-story rope tunnel immediately snares the attention of older visitors, though there are several age-appropriate attractions for children, from infants to pre-teens.

## 4 Wrigley Field

A baseball-lover's park, Wrigley Field *(p89)* is a small and intimate stadium that's far less intimidating for children than many larger stadia. A ticket to anywhere in the grandstand allows you to walk around the playing field and get to the rooftop terrace: the outfield stands can get rowdy, but a neighboring family section bans the beer that fuels the "bleacher bums." After Sunday games, children can even run the bases on the field.

**Saltwater habitat at the Abbott Oceanarium, Shedd Aquarium**

## 5 Shedd Aquarium

Opened in 1930, the Shedd Aquarium *(p36)* is housed in a Neo-Classical building overlooking Lake Michigan. Its Abbott Oceanarium is home to beluga whales and dolphins, while Wild Reef recreates a vibrant coral reef and is home to sharks and other large marine animals. In the Polar Play Zone, kids can don a penguin suit and waddle in the Icy South play area or explore Arctic waters in the Icy North in a kids' size submarine.

## 6 Lincoln Park Zoo

One of the country's only free-admission zoos, Lincoln Park Zoo *(p90)* is easily accessible from Downtown. The zoo is a leading light for ape research, and its park setting, duck ponds, historic café, and landmark red barn endear it to all who visit. In summer, a motorized "train" makes a scenic loop around the park, while on the pond, paddleboats float among the ducks.

## 7 Field Museum

Packed with attractions for the whole family, the Field Museum *(p28)* features giant dinosaurs like SUE the T. rex, Egyptian tombs and mummies, gemstones and geodes, 3D movies, and the hands-on Crown Family PlayLab for little ones. Check the museum calendar for special events for kids of all ages, from fossil workshops to art classes.

## 8 Chicago River Boat Tours

Children will love a boat ride on the Chicago River, floating among the towering skyscrapers and listening to stories of the city and how the river's flow was reversed to spare Lake Michigan its pollution *(p9)*. Wendella and Shoreline Sightseeing *(shoreline sightseeing.com)* both have tours that embark from Michigan Avenue, and feature family-friendly narration, from spring through to fall.

## 9 Navy Pier

Kids make a beeline for Navy Pier's *(p34)* traditional carnival rides, which includes a 196-ft- (60-m-) high Ferris wheel and musical carousel. The ships that line the docks, from sleek, tall-masted schooners to powerful motor-boats, also grab their attention. Families enjoy thrilling time amid hundreds of live butterflies at The Butterfly House. All restaurants here are family friendly.

## 10 Griffin Museum of Science and Industry

Though this museum *(p30)* dazzles kids and adults alike with its submarine ship and replica coal mine, it's The Idea Factory that's designed just for juniors. With the pulling of gears and shifting of knobs, kids experiment through play with balance, construction, magnetism, and more. A current-fed waterway encourages boat building.

# LOCAL DISHES

### 1 Deep-dish Pizza

For decades, Chicago has been known as the home of deep-dish pizza, a thick-crust variation of the Italian classic with mounds of melted cheese, and a generous helping of tomato sauce. While its origins are heavily contested, there are numerous great spots today with their own take on the now iconic dish, including Gino's East *(ginoseast.com)*, Lou Malnati's *(lou malnatis.com)*, and Pizzeria Uno *(p87)*.

### 2 Chicago-style Hot Dog

The Chicago version of this quick and easy meal is little changed since it was first brought to the city by 19th-century European immigrants. Its recipe is simple: an all-beef frankfurter on a poppy-seed bun, topped with seven ingredients – mustard (but no ketchup), relish, onion, tomato slices, a pickle spear, sport peppers, and celery salt. Find them at fixtures across town, such as Devil Dawgs *(devildawgs.com)* and Superdawg *(superdawg.com)*. For a truly Chicago experience, grab one at the ballpark to enjoy with the game.

### 3 Italian Beef Sandwich

The chunky sandwich has long been a Chicago favorite, but is now a global icon thanks to the TV series *The Bear*. It's comprised of thinly sliced roast beef and gravy, all squeezed into a long French roll and generally topped with peppers or another vegetable. Try the sandwich the TV show is based on at Mr. Beef *(p87)*, or seek out other top variations at spots like Al's *(alsbeef.com)* and Portillo's *(portillos.com)*.

### 4 Chicago Mix Popcorn

Cheese and caramel. Perhaps not the obvious popcorn mixture, but thanks to Garrett *(garrettpopcorn.com)* and Nuts on Clark *(nutsonclark.com)*, it's become a favorite snack among Chicagoans. You may have to get in line to enjoy some, but it's worth the wait.

### 5 Chicago-style BBQ

Many regions in the US have their own version of BBQ, and Chicago is no exception (no surprise given the city's history as a meatpacking hub). Places like Smoque *(p95)* still shine a light on

**Queuing for Garrett's signature Chicago Mix Popcorn**

**Rows of powder-topped *paczki*, Polish sweet treats**

options that are easier on the wallet and full of flavor, with local specialties such as rib tips and hot links, served typically with a sweet, tangy sauce.

## 6 Paczki

Chicago is home to the largest Polish population in America, and with that culture has come flavorful treats. The most famous is *paczki*, deep-fried doughballs, filled with fruit or cream, and topped with powdered sugar. They are found in bakeries across the city, particularly during March when they are traditionally sold on Fat Tuesday, also known as Paczki day in Chicago, as a way to use up ingredients before Lent.

## 7 Croissants

While the croissant has French origins, the *viennoiserie* has taken on an identity of its own in Chicago, with pastry chefs putting their own spin on this morning staple. The flaky offerings at Floriole *(floriole.com)* are divine – try the ham and cheese – as are the black truffle croissants at Kasama *(kasamachicago.com)*. For the classic, it's hard to beat Lost Larson *(lostlarson.com)*.

## 8 Burgers

Chicago has had a long love affair with burgers: some claim the first hamburger in the US was served here in 1917, and the first McDonald's franchise was opened in the suburb of Des Plaines. The range has expanded since then and now includes everything from griddled patties to tasty veggie options. Some of the best-loved are those at The Loyalist *(smythandtheloyalist.com)*, Au Cheval *(p81)*, and Billy Goat Tavern (a classic, with layers of meat and cheese, *p87*).

## 9 Saganaki

There are few better ways to start a meal than with this flaming Greek appetizer, which is reputed to have originated at the Parthenon restaurant in Greektown. It's a fairly simple cheese dish – a crispy, fried outside with melted cheese inside – but is spectacularly flambéed right at your table, complete with the exclaimed "Opa!" Nowadays, most spots in Greektown have both the dish and the show – you can't go wrong with the version at Greek Islands *(greekislands.net)*.

## 10 Malört

While a drink, this bracing, polarizing wormwood liqueur is as tethered to Chicago's food identity as deep-dish pizza and hot dogs. Swedish immigrant Carl Jeppson introduced it in the 1930s and it has spread across the city, with many bars serving a drink that's now known as a "bartender's handshake."

**A many-layered Chicago-style burger**

# PERFORMANCE VENUES

## 1 Lyric Opera of Chicago

J4 20 N. Wacker Dr.
lyricopera.org

Established in 1954, the Lyric Opera is among the leading companies in the US, drawing the top singers and directors. From September through May it offers a mix of classical operas, modern premieres, and some of the more popular musicals, most of which are performed at the ornate Art Deco Civic Opera House *(p79)*.

## 2 Chicago Symphony Orchestra

Founded in 1891, this orchestra performs classical and contemporary pieces, with pop culture programs such as film scores thrown in. Its main home is the magnificent Symphony Center *(p79)*, but in the summer, they play at the outdoor suburban venue, Ravinia. Finnish conductor Klaus Mäkelä was named music director-designate in 2024, with his first official season set to begin in 2027.

## 3 Court Theater

E5 5535 S. Ellis Ave.
courttheatre.org

This theater traces its roots to three Molière productions performed at the University of Chicago in 1955. The Court still mounts many classics, but it varies its seasons with musicals like *Guys and Dolls* and literary adaptations such as James Joyce's *The Dead*.

## 4 Steppenwolf Theater Co.

Established in 1974 in a church basement, Steppenwolf *(p90)* has gained acclaim based on the fame of its ensemble, which has included actors Gary Sinise, Joan Allen, Carrie Coon, and Jon Michael Hill. Though the company has moved to a specially built theater in Lincoln Park, it is still distinguished by raw emotion and edgy productions, and has received many notable accolades, including several Tony® Awards.

## 5 Chicago Shakespeare Theater

M3 800 E. Grand Ave.
chicagoshakes.com

This Navy Pier venue presents a dynamic space for Shakespeare's repertory. Its 510-seat courtyard design is inspired by the original layout in traditional playhouses

**Performers receiving a standing ovation at the Court Theater**

**Entrance to the Chicago Shakespeare Theater**

of the Bard's day. Visiting non-Shakespeare productions take place after the company's September-to-April season.

## 6 Goodman Theater

K3 170 N. Dearborn St.
goodmantheatre.org

One of Chicago's leading theater companies, the Goodman has put on many top shows over the years andfrequently spins off productions to Broadway in New York, many of which have earned Tony® Awards. Noted shows include dramas by Eugene O'Neill such as *The Iceman Cometh* and *Two Trains Running* by August Wilson, and an annual version of Charles Dickens' *A Christmas Carol*.

## 7 Second City

Since 1959, Chicago's famed Second City *(p91)* comedy troupe has launched such comic lights as Tina Fey, Amy Poehler, and Bill Murray. Reservations are a must.

## 8 Lookingglass Theater

L2 163 E. Pearson St.
lookingglasstheatre.org

In 1988, eight Northwestern University students, including *Friends* actor David Schwimmer, founded Lookingglass, a bold company incorporating dance, circus arts, and live music in its original theatrical productions.

## 9 The Joffrey Ballet

J4 10 E. Randolph St.
joffrey.org

This world-class ballet company was formed in 1956, taking up residence in Chicago in 1995. Its main season runs from September to June. Performances are held at the Lyric Opera House and feature classics such as *Carmen* and *The Nutcracker*.

## 10 Old Town School of Folk Music

E3 4544 N. Lincoln Ave.
oldtownschool.org

Since the 1950s the Old Town School has brought world and homegrown folk music performers to Chicago. Its home in Lincoln Square opened in 1998 with a concert by Joni Mitchell, though you're more likely to catch a women's ensemble from Mali and contemporary folkies. Over 6,000 students are enrolled in its music programs held every week.

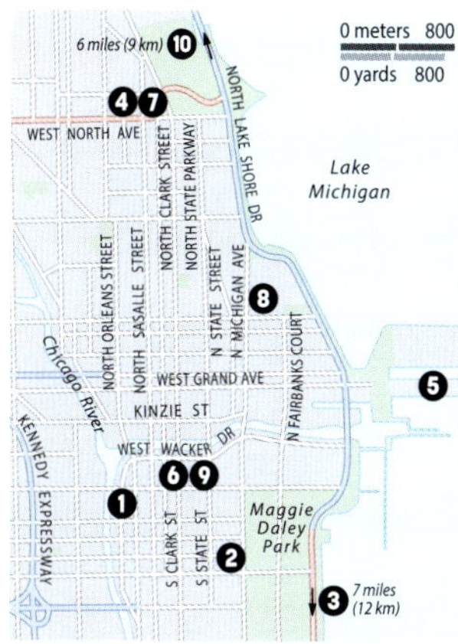

# NIGHTS OUT

## 1 Comedy

As the birthplace of improv comedy, Chicago is home to some of America's premier comedy theaters, with famous institutions such as Second City *(p91)* and iO *(ioimprov.com)*. Both still churn out belly laughs on a nightly basis with their hilarious shows. To see the best in up-and-coming comedic talent, catch a show at Lincoln Lodge *(thelincolnlodge.com)* or the Den *(thedentheatre.com)*.

## 2 Jazz and Blues Bars

Jazz and blues have been an indelible part of Chicago's culture for over a century, and this has created a "Chicago sound" that's unique to the city. Andy's Jazz Club *(andysjazzclub.com)* is a great place for an introduction to the jazz scene, and serves lovely Cajun fare, while Jazz Showcase *(jazzshowcase.com)* is a venue that's been drawing the best musicians (Count Basie and Dizzy Gillespie included) since 1947. If it's the blues you're after, check out the high-energy shows at Blue Chicago *(bluechicago.com)* or the late-night sets at Kingston Mines *(kingstonmines.com)*.

**Musicians performing in Andy's Jazz Club**

## 3 Rooftop Bars

If you want the best views in town as the sun goes down, Chicago's array of rooftop bars has you covered. Get a new perspective of the city's skyline with a cocktail in hand at Cindy's *(p81)*, or look down on the always bustling Michigan Avenue from NoMI Garden *(p87)*. For the ultimate view of both Chicago and Lake Michigan, check out Offshore *(p35)* in Navy Pier – it's home to the largest rooftop bar in the world.

## 4 Trivia Nights

Fancy yourself a trivia master? Test your skills against locals at a trivia night, many of which are run by "America's best team trivia game," Whaddayaknow Trivia. Head to George St Pub *(gspchicago.com)* on Wednesdays for its Drafts and Trivia night or try aliveOne *(aliveone.com)* for its Monday music trivia night (return on Tuesday for music bingo).

## 5 Live Music

With tons of bars and venues *(p62)*, there's always a variety of places to hear live music in Chicago. Many neighborhood bars have great local acts who perform regularly, but if you want to see the stars in action, hit up marquee venues such as Chicago Theater *(p78)*, Thalia Hall *(p100)*, and the Salt Shed *(saltshedchicago.com)*. If you prefer your concerts alfresco, check out the summer series at Ravinia or the varied festivals in Millennium Park *(p42)*.

## 6 Cocktail Bars

Chicago has no shortage of cocktail bars serving up wonderful creations, so you're well catered for no matter how you take your drink. Highlights include the tropical flavors at the tiki bar in Three Dots and a Dash *(threedotschicago.com)*, drinks that look more like science experiments at The Aviary *(theaviary.com)*, and The Alderman *(thealdermanchicago.com)*, where the intimate setting evokes the days of speakeasies.

**The facade of Chicago Theater**

## 7 Craft Breweries

Chicago is the place to be for beer connoisseurs. It's home to over 160 craft breweries, each with its own style and taste, so there's plenty of suds to sink. There's a range of IPAs, pale ales, and seasonal brews at the Half Acre *(halfacrebeer.com)*, 18 on-tap beers at Goose Island *(p94)*, and more unusual concoctions at Off Color *(offcolorbrewing.com)*.

## 8 Museum Lates

Many of Chicago's best cultural sites offer up regular late-night treats for those seeking an evening of culture. Visitors can discover the wonders of space every Wednesday night at the Adler Planetarium *(p97)* or explore the exhibitions at the Field Museum *(p28)* until 9pm at its once-a-month after-hours event. Kids are well catered for, too: both the Griffin Museum of Science and Industry *(p30)* and the Field Museum hold sleepover events throughout the year for families with kids aged 6-12.

## 9 Theater

Chicago has long been home to a rich and diverse theater scene, with everything from Broadway productions to new creations from up-and-coming stars. Broadway shows are performed at several central theaters including the Cadillac Palace Theatre *(cadillacpalacetheatre.com)* and the CIBC Theatre *(18 W Monroe St)*, while independent theaters, such as the Steppenwolf Theatre *(p90)* and Court Theatre *(p62)*, put on some of the finest new productions in the US.

## 10 See the Big Game

Chicago is home to professional teams from a wide variety of sports *(p71)*, so no matter what time of year you arrive, you're guaranteed to see world-class sports stars in action. There are few more pleasurable activities than a summer evening at the ballpark, and Chicago is home to two baseball teams, the Cubs and the White Sox. At other times, you can catch the Bears play an NFL game at the historic Soldier Field *(p23)* or see either the Bulls play basketball or the Blackhawks play ice hockey at the United Center *(p23)*.

**An aerial view of the NFL stadium, Soldier Field**

# SHOPPING DESTINATIONS

## 1 The Magnificent Mile

This stretch of North Michigan Avenue is one of the city's retail hubs *(p40)*. Besides sophisticated designer boutiques, there are malls (each with high-end department stores), big-name chains, and flagship stores.

## 2 Oak Street

L1

If you have to ask how much it costs, you should probably plan on just window-shopping along this stretch of Chicago's upper-crust Gold Coast, bordered by North Michigan Avenue and Rush Street. Boutiques here sell designer wear, accessories, and include some shops exclusive to Chicago such as Razny Jewelers, known for its bespoke jewelry, and Swiss-made watches.

## 3 Andersonville

B3

This far Northside neighborhood, between Foster and Bryn Mawr avenues, hosts a string of independent boutiques along the bustling Clark Street. The area is a must-visit for those looking for vintage or eco-friendly products. Zoning regulations have kept out the big-box stores with the result that the bookshops, galleries, design stores, and clothing specialists offer unique goods.

## 4 Bucktown Neighborhood

B4

Bordered by Fullerton Avenue to the north and Bloomingdale Avenue to the south, with the Kennedy Expressway (I-94) cutting through the middle, Bucktown was once a hotspot for artists. Today, the area is packed with clothing stores, edgy music shops, and high-end designer boutiques.

## 5 WoodField Mall

Woodfield Mall, Schaumburg
10am–8pm daily (to 9pm Fri & Sat, to 6pm Sun) simon.com/mall/woodfield-mall

The largest shopping mall in the Chicago metro area, Woodfield is about 25 miles (40 km) northwest of downtown. This sprawling complex features over 220 stores, with popular high-street favorites, like Nordstrom, Zara, Macy's, Gap, and Apple.

## 6 Broadway Antique Market

E2 6130 N. Broadway
11am–7pm Mon–Sat, 11am–6pm Sun

An old-time movie palace sign indicates the 1939 building that houses this market. With 75 dealers stocking artwork, jewelry, clothing, and more in styles such as Art Deco, and Mid-Century Modern, you are sure to find something to suit.

Sleek facade of the Burberry store on the Magnificent Mile

## 7 Pilsen

B5

Nestled between West 16th Street, South Ashland Avenue, and the Chicago River, this primarily Mexican-American neighborhood lies southwest of downtown. Most of the action happens along 18th Street, where you'll find not only cantinas and taquerias but also a variety of shops like Knee Deep, Pilsen Vintage, and Mestiza, which offers Mexican gifts.

## 8 Hyde Park

F5

This Southside neighborhood, framed by South Cottage Grove Avenue, East Hyde Park Avenue, and Lake Michigan, is a perfect place to shop. Highlights include 57th Street Books, Toys et Cetera and the Silverroom, offering jewelry, fashion, and art.

## 9 Armitage Avenue

E4

This street in Lincoln Park is a favorite for those who are seeking out-of-the-ordinary clothing, home decor, bath and body products – and don't mind spending more to get it.

## 10 State Street

Home to landmark department stores, this area *(p77)* offers something for everyone. Macy's *(p80)* satisfies every shopper's needs, while TJ Maxx *(p80)* has low prices and extensive variety.

Famous department store Macy's on State Street

## TOP 10 MARKETS

Novelties at a Christkindlmarket

**1. Swap-O-Rama Flea Markets**
swap-o-rama.com
A popular weekend flea market with three convenient locations.

**2. Green City Market Lincoln Park**
F3 1817 N. Clark
greencitymarket.org
Open from April to October, this is the city's largest fresh produce market.

**3. Maxwell Street Market**
This century-old market *(p99)* is known for its eclectic stalls and live music.

**4. Sauced Night Market**
saucedmarket.com
A traveling night market with live DJs, food stalls, and local goods.

**5. Wicker Park Farmers Market**
B4 1425 N. Damen Ave.
A seasonal farmers' Sunday market.

**6. The Buyers Flea Market**
J1 454 W. Division St.
buyersfleamarket.com
An indoor market with diverse wares.

**7. Randolph Street Market**
J4 1341 W. Randolph St.
randolphstreetmarket.com
A seasonal antiques market.

**8. Vintage House Chicago**
B4 vintagehousechicago.com
A bi-montly vintage and crafts market.

**9. Chicago Artisan Market**
H5 and B3 chicagoartisansmarket.com
A craft market with over 100 artisans.

**10. Christkindlmarket**
G4 50 W. Washington St
christkindlmarket.com
This is Chicago's largest open-air christmas market, held in Daley Plaza.

# CHICAGO FOR FREE

**Enjoying a live performance at Millennium Park**

## 1 Millennium Park

During the summer, Millennium Park *(p42)* hosts a series of free events and performances, including concerts by the Lyric Opera of Chicago *(p62)* and Uniting Voices Chicago, as well as screenings of popular films.

## 2 Navy Pier

Navy Pier *(p34)* offers one of the most scenic strolls in Chicago, with a carnival-like atmosphere and myriad attractions. Entry to the pier is free, as are the dazzling fireworks displays held on Wednesday and Saturday nights through the summer.

## 3 Lincoln Park Zoo

One of the last free zoos in the country, Lincoln Park Zoo *(p90)* is a leader in wildlife conservation, actively working to protect endangered species. It is home to more than 1,000 mammals, reptiles, and birds.

## 4 Public Art

Many famous artists, such as Pablo Picasso, Alexander Calder, and Marc Chagall have left their artistic mark on the city. Details of public art downtown are included in the Loop Sculpture Guide, downloadable from cityofchicago.org.

## 5 Free Events

Summer in Chicago brings lots of free outdoor festivals *(chicago.gov/city/en/depts/dca.html)*, from the big music events of Grant Park, such as the Chicago Blues Festival *(p70)*, to parades, circuses in the parks, and neighborhood festivals that feature entertainment and food and drink vendors.

## 6 Comedy Shows

Chicago is the place to catch the best rising comedy and improv stars. The iO Theater runs dozens of shows each week from its Near North headquarters, some of them free and all of them a blast. Also check Comedy Sportz *(malarkeycomedy.com)* for freebies.

## 7 Lakefront Recreational Path

This 18-mile (29-km) paved path along Lake Michigan is popular for running, cycling, skating, and walking. On busy summer days, it sees more than 50,000 visitors, making it one of the city's most visited thoroughfares. Many hotels can supply rental bicycles and the city's bike-share program Divvy *(divvybikes.com)* offers cheap wheels.

**Strolling along the Lakefront Recreational Path**

## 8 Lincoln Park Conservatory and Gardens

This elegant 19th-century tropical conservatory *(p90)* comprises four display houses: the Palm House, Fern Room, Orchid House, and Show House, each filled with exotic flowers and thousands of plants. While admission is free, visitors must reserve timed-entry tickets in advance.

## 9 Free Museums

A number of smaller museums across Chicago offer free admission, including the National Museum of Mexican Art *(p50)*, the National Museum of Puerto Rican Arts & Culture *(nmprac.org)*, the National Veterans Art Museum *(p50)*, the Museum of Contemporary Photography *(p98)*, the Smart Museum of Art *(smartmuseum.uchicago.edu)*, the Jane Addams Hull-House Museum *(p99)*, and the fascinating Mindworks: The Science of Thinking *(chicagobooth.edu/mindworks)*.

## 10 Free Tours

The tourism bureau Choose Chicago *(choosechicago.com)* offers visitors free guided tours led by locals. To join a Chicago Greeter *(chicagogreeter.com)* tour – lasting two to four hours – sign up on its website at least ten days in advance. InstaGreeters *(Chicagogreeter.com)* are also available for tours spanning an hour from Friday to Sunday.

## TOP 10 **BUDGET TIPS**

**1.** See the city on a Divvy Bike. A 30-minute ride costs $6.50, or get a day pass for $18.10 and enjoy three hour of riding within 24 hours.

**2.** Many restaurants offer good-value "Early Bird Specials" or pre-theater menus. Look for signs advertising these deals throughout the city.

**3.** Chicago's many beautiful parks offer free skating rinks, beaches, pools, tennis courts, and walking and cycling paths. These spaces are frequented by locals and visitors alike.

**4.** Choose Chicago offers several promotional discounts, such as Winter Delights, which include discounts on lodging, attractions, and meals.

**5.** Chicago's CityPass *(p117)* grants 50 percent off on tickets, for entry to five top attractions including the Shedd Aquarium *(p36)*, the Skydeck, and the Field Museum *(p28)*.

**6.** Last-minute tickets for the current week's theater performances can be purchased online at hottix.org or by calling 312-977-9483. Discounted rates are offered for many of these performances.

**7.** Ring the Loop aboard the Brown Line "L" running out to Lincoln Park *(p55)* and back again for a scenic tour at just $2.50.

**8.** Look out for neighborhood restaurants that offer a BYOB service, and bring your own alcoholic drinks to enjoy with your dinner.

**9.** Find cheap deals on Chicago's famous deep-dish pizza: Lou Malnati's *(loumalnatis.com)* offers a $5 happy hour (3–5:30pm Mon–Fri), while Gino's East *(ginoseast.com)* has lunch specials for $12.79.

**10.** Make a trip to the Chicago Cultural Center *(p75)* to admire its stained-glass dome, and to enjoy some of the free concerts that are regularly scheduled here.

# FESTIVALS AND EVENTS

## 1 Chicago Summer Neighborhood Festivals

May–Sep W choosechicago.com

Chicago has upwards of 100 neighborhood festivals. Virtually every summer weekend features an event or three, ranging from the Northalsted Market Days to the Taste of Korea.

## 2 Chicago Blues Festival

Early Jun

The raucous weekend-long Blues Festival kicks off summer in Chicago. About 750,000 listeners converge at the Millennium Park for the world's largest free blues event. Its main stage hosts traditional blues and gospel performers like Mavis Staples, jazz interpreters such as Mose Allison, and blues-inflected artists like Bonnie Raitt. Smaller side stages offer a more intimate experience.

## 3 Chicago Pride Fest

Jun W pridechicago.org

Annual LGBTQ+ celebrations, including the colorful Pride Parade and the Chicago Pride Fest, take place in the city every June. Based around Northalsted, the month-long festivities culminate in a two-day street festival that draws huge crowds.

## 4 Old Town Art Fair

Jun W oldtownartfair.org

This 50-year-old fair transforms the lanes of Old Town with over 200 artist booths, offering a mix of food vendors, children's entertainment, and garden tours.

## 5 Lollapalooza

Late Jul W lollapalooza.com

Created by Perry Farrell, lead vocalist of Jane's Addiction, this popular four-day rock festival was first held in 1991. Held in Grant Park in late July, it has featured major headliners like Paul McCartney and Olivia Rodrigo, alongside emerging rockers, DJs, and techno artists performing across multiple stages. Passes go on sale in March and usually sell out quickly.

## 6 Chicago Air and Water Show

Mid-Aug

Since 1959, this impressive display of military power has taken place along the shores of Lake Michigan. The show features historic aircraft flybys, a staged amphibious attack, and precision flying teams. Prime viewing spots stretch from Oak Street to Montrose Beach.

Christmas Parade at North Michigan Avenue

## 7 Chicago Jazz Festival

Late Aug/early Sep (including Labor Day weekend)

The Jazz Fest caps summer, when music fans are drawn to Millennium Park for free concerts by greats like Branford Marsalis and Roy Hargrove.

## 8 Taste of Chicago

Early Sep

Chicago's signature foods take center stage during the long weekend Taste of Chicago festival. Held in Grant Park, the festival also features live musical performances, a carnival with rides, and cooking demonstrations.

## 9 World Music Festival

Late Sep–early Oct W chicago.gov/city/en/depts/dca/supp_info/wmf.html

This city-wide, multi-venue, week-long festival showcases the very best of traditional and contemporary international music. Concerts are low-cost or even free.

## 10 The Magnificent Mile Holiday Lights Festival

Mid-Nov–end Dec

One of the biggest Christmas holiday festivities in the US, this daylong celebration kicks off the season with beautifully decorated shops and trees along Michigan Avenue. The tree-lighting parade and fireworks display over the Chicago River is held just before Thanksgiving.

Contrails during the Chicago Air and Water Show

## TOP 10 SPORTS TEAMS

**1. Chicago Bears**
W chicagobears.com
This team plays at the Soldier Field *(p23)* from September to December.

**2. Chicago Cubs**
The baseball games of the 2016 Series champions at the Wrigley Stadium *(p89)* are often a sell-out.

**3. Chicago White Sox**
W mlb.com/whitesox
The White Sox are famed for their rivalry with the Chicago Cubs.

**4. Chicago Bulls**
W nba.com/bulls
The city's basketball team plays at the United Center *(p22)*.

**5. Chicago Blackhawks**
W nhl.com/blackhawks
The Stanley Cup-winning NHL team shares the United Center *(p22)* with the Bulls.

**6. Chicago Sky**
W sky.wnba.com
Winners of the 2021 WNBA, this team plays from May to September at the WinTrust Arena.

**7. Chicago Fire**
W chicagofirefc.com
The Fire MLS soccer team shares Soldier Field with the Bears, with the season running from April to October.

**8. Chicago Wolves**
W chicagowolves.com
Five-time American Hockey League champions, the Chicago Wolves offer an exciting evening of ice hockey from October to May.

**9. Chicago Hounds**
W chicagohounds.com
Catch the city's Major League Rugby team in action at the SeatGeek Stadium from February to July.

**10. Chicago Stars**
W chicagostars.com
This women's NWSL soccer team is always a thrill to watch at the SeatGeek Stadium. The season runs from March to October.

# AREA BY AREA



*A Chicago suburb at sunset*

# THE LOOP

Named for the ring of elevated train tracks that encircle it, this is downtown Chicago's core, and the city's financial and governmental hub. Abuzz with laptop-toting businesspeople during the week, the area transforms on weekends when a veritable shopping frenzy erupts along its famous State Street. Those craving some culture come flocking to see the collections of the Art Institute of Chicago and to enjoy its notable public art, as well as the area's many architecturally significant buildings. The surrounding public parks offer green recreational spaces and the Chicago Riverwalk pedestrian path is a great place for strolling. The area is also known for its lively nightlife, thanks to its vibrant theater district, offering a variety of shows, and many lovely bars and restaurants.

*For places to stay in this area, see p118*

Stained-glass dome at the Chicago Cultural Center

## 1 Chicago Cultural Center

L4 78 E. Washington St. 312-744-6630 10am–5pm daily

Built in 1897 as the city's first main library, this magnificent Beaux-Arts building was described at the time as the "people's palace." In 1991, the library moved out, allowing several galleries, performance spaces, and a visitor information center to move in. Guided tours offer a historical overview of the building, which occupies an entire block and has one of the world's largest domes, designed by American Art Nouveau artist L. C. Tiffany, and rooms modeled after the Doge's Palace in Venice and the Acropolis in Athens.

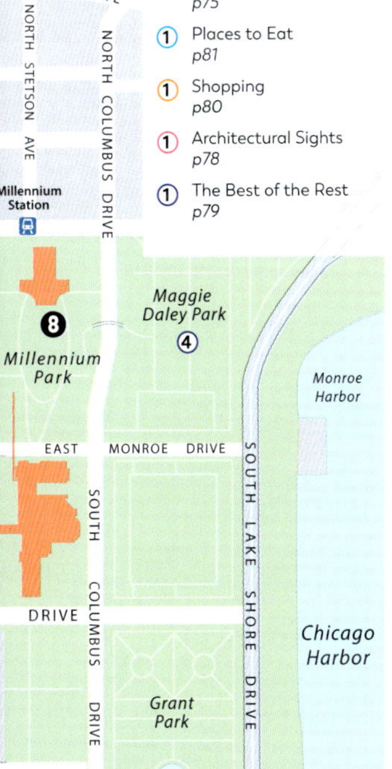


## 2 Chicago Board of Trade (CBOT)

K5 141 W. Jackson Blvd.

The Chicago Board of Trade (CBOT) was founded in 1848 to create a central marketplace in the fast-developing city, and moved to its present 45-story home in 1930. Designed by the famous architectural firm Holabird and Root, it is a stunning example of Art Deco. Capping the limestone building is a huge statue of Ceres, the Roman goddess of grain and harvest. A 23-story glass-and-steel addition designed by Helmut Jahn was added in 1980. Tours of the building can be booked through the Chicago Architecture Center *(p113)*.

## 3 Willis Tower

An architectural superlative, the tower *(p22)* offers superb views from its 103rd-floor Skydeck where you'll find yourself atop 222,500 tons of steel.

## 4 The Art Institute of Chicago

This extraordinary collection *(p24)* spans over 4,000 years of international art, much of it donated by wealthy Chicago collectors.

Bronze lion statue at the Art Institute of Chicago

## 5 The Rookery

**K4 209 S. LaSalle St. 7am–6pm Mon–Fri, 8am–2pm Sat**

This 11-story building, with its rusticated red granite base, was the country's largest office building and a precursor to modern skyscrapers when it was completed in 1888 by architects Daniel H. Burnham *(p49)* and John Root. Its stunning Light Court was redesigned in 1907 by Frank Lloyd Wright *(p49)*, who added a grand staircase and hanging light fixtures, both of which carry his signature circle-in-square motif.

### THE LOOP'S SCULPTURE

Setting a trend for public artwork downtown, Pablo Picasso's untitled sculpture, simply known as *the Picasso*, was donated to Chicago in 1967. The Loop's street corners now feature more than 100 sculptures, mosaics, and murals by established as well as upcoming artists. A guide to the open-air artworks can be downloaded from cityofchicago.org.

## 6 Harold Washington Library Center

**K5 400 S. State St. 9am–8pm Mon–Thu, 9am–5pm Fri & Sat, 1–5pm Sun chipublib.org/locations/34**

Named after Harold Washington, Chicago's first African American mayor, this is the largest public library building in the country. Its collections, which include a superlative Blues Archive and a massive children's library, fill an incredible 70 miles (110 km) of shelving. Architects Hammond, Beeby, and Babka incorporated architectural elements of several Chicago landmarks, such as the Rookery and the Art Institute of Chicago *(p75)* in the building's design: don't miss the ninth-floor Winter Garden atrium, which soars two stories to a spectacular glass dome.

## 7 Chicago Riverwalk

Running along the south bank of the Chicago River, beginning near Lake Michigan, the Chicago Riverwalk *(p38)* is a scenic waterside walkway. Its bike and pedestrian paths are great spots for spying the skyscrapers lining the river, and for picnicking. Along the way, there are restaurants, a floating garden, and boat and bike rentals. The section from State to LaSalle has amphitheater-like seating and an area for kayak launches.

## 8 Millennium Park

The modern Millennium Park *(p42)* is Chicago's superb adaptation of its "front yard." The park is home to a dynamic Frank Gehry-designed music pavilion and pedestrian bridge, and a vast sculpture, *Cloud Gate* (aka "The Bean"), by British artist Anish Kapoor. It also houses lush gardens, restaurants, a winter ice rink, peristyle, an interactive fountain by Spanish artist Jaume Plensa, and the city's iconic art museum, the Art Institute of Chicago *(p24)*. The adjoining Grant Park *(p23)* is also a popular spot, hosting many summer festivals such as the Taste of Chicago *(p71)*. It is home to the Museum Campus and the elaborate Buckingham Fountain, dating to 1927.

## 9 The "L"

Originally called the Union Loop, this system of elevated trains *(p113)* came about after the 1871 Great Chicago Fire when the city was rebuilt with such unexpected success that, within 20 years, its streets could no longer handle the influx of people, streetcars, and horses filling them. Today, four lines ring the business district – the Orange, Purple, Pink, and Brown lines – with three others connecting it to places farther afield.

## 10 State Street

K4

This "great street" got its nickname from a famous line in Fred Fisher's 1922 hit song *Chicago*. Although it didn't always live up to this catchy moniker, it has won back many fans since its face-lift in 1996. It now sports replica Art Deco lampposts and subway entrances, and was on the National Register of Historic Places. This lively stretch, between Wacker Drive and Ida B. Wells Drive, has shopping, history, education, architecture, theater, and dining. The atmosphere is especially merry when the Thanksgiving parade brings Santa to town.

**Strolling along the river's edge, Chicago Riverwalk**

### A DAY IN THE LOOP

#### Morning

Start early with breakfast at the **Drawing Room** *(drawingroomchicago.com)*, off the lobby of the historic **Chicago Athletic Association** hotel *(p118)*. Stroll across the street to **Millennium Park** *(p42)*, to see the **Cloud Gate** sculpture, the video-screen fountains, and the Lurie Garden. From the park, take the pedestrian bridge designed by Renzo Piano, directly to the **Art Institute of Chicago** *(p24)*. A whirlwind tour of the highlights, located on the upper level and in the Modern Wing, takes a couple of hours. Have lunch at **The Modern Bar**, on the second floor of the Modern Wing, and enjoy people-watching over the main hall.

#### Afternoon

Next, stroll up N. Columbus Drive to spend time meandering along the **Chicago Riverwalk**. Be sure to stop by the **Chicago Architecture Center** *(111 E. Wacker Dr.)*, which has a lovely shop stocked with design-related souvenirs. After, walk down nearby State Street, stopping to browse the shops. Book a pre-theater table at **Petterino's** *(p81)*, an old-school supper club, then check out the show at the **Goodman Theater** *(p63)* next door. End the day by heading to the **Chicago Athletic Association** for a nightcap at **Cindy's** *(p81)* rooftop bar.

# Architectural Sights

**Beaux Arts-style Chicago Theater by Rapp & Rapp**

### 1. Monadnock Building

K5 53 W. Jackson Blvd.

At 16 stories, this impressive 1891 edifice is one of the world's tallest all-masonry high-rises. Designed by the architectural firm Holabird and Roche (now Holabird and Root), it features a grand wrought-iron staircase inside.

### 2. Marquette Building

K4 140 S. Dearborn St.

Holabird and Roche built this Chicago School structure with a steel skeleton and decorative ornamentation in 1895.

### 3. Fisher Building

K5 343 S. Dearborn St.

This 1896 Neo-Gothic building, designed by Daniel H. Burnham, is considered a masterpiece of the Chicago School and was designated a city landmark in 1978. Its steel facade features aquatic motifs that pay tribute to the building's first owner, L. G. Fisher.

### 4. One North LaSalle

K4

This 1930-built, 49-story building was Chicago's tallest for 35 years, and is one of the city's best surviving examples of Art Deco architecture.

### 5. Santa Fe Center

L6 224 S. Michigan Ave.

Beaux Arts architect Daniel H. Burnham designed this elegant high-rise in 1904. Its carved building signs are from Chicago's days as a railroad hub.

### 6. Chicago Theater

K4 175 N. State St.

The red sign of this Beaux Arts theater is a symbol of Chicago. Built in 1921 as a movie theater, today it is a performance venue.

### 7. Reliance Building

K4 1 W. Washington St.

Daniel H. Burnham's stunning 1895 building, featuring glass and white-glazed terracotta, is now home to the Alise Chicago hotel.

### 8. Sullivan Center

K4 1 S. State St.

The cast-iron swirls on the exterior of this building, constructed between 1899 and 1903, showcase architect Louis H. Sullivan's passion for detail.

### 9. Inland Steel Building

K4 30 W. Monroe St.

One of the first skyscrapers to be built in 1957, with steel, not concrete, pilings, this predates the John Hancock Center *(p83)* in using external supports.

### 10. Federal Center

K4 219 S. Dearborn St.

Flanked by Modernist federal buildings designed by architect and interior designer Ludwig Mies van der Rohe, this plaza houses Alexander Calder's striking 53-ft (16-m) red steel statue, *Flamingo* (1974).

# The Best of the Rest

### 1. Loop Theater District

K4

A sidewalk plaque at Randolph and State streets denotes Chicago's officially designated Theater District, a cluster of old and new theaters.

### 2. Civic Opera House

J4 20 N. Wacker Dr. lyricopera.org

This 1929 structure was inspired by Paris's Opera Garnier. It is home to the Lyric Opera of Chicago *(p62)*.

### 3. Old St. Patrick's Church

J4 700 W. Adams St.

Chicago's oldest church, built in 1856, is crowned by two towers – one Romanesque, the other Byzantine – symbolizing East and West.

### 4. Maggie Daley Park

L4 37 E. Randolph St.

If Millennium Park is about art, its neighbor is all about play. It includes a playground, climbing walls, tennis courts, and a winter skating ribbon.

### 5. Symphony Center

L4 220 S. Michigan Ave. cso.org

At the heart of this center is the Orchestra Hall, home of the Chicago Symphony Orchestra.

### 6. Chicago Temple

J4 77 W. Washington St.

A Gothic-inspired structure designed by Holabird and Roche in 1923. Under the majestic spire is a 35-seat chapel.

### 7. Federal Reserve Bank

K4 230 S. LaSalle St.

This impressive edifice is one of 12 regional Reserve banks. When it was first built in 1922, it had the largest bank vaults ever constructed.

### 8. American Writers Museum

L4 180 N. Michigan Ave. americanwritersmuseum.org

America's rich literary history is celebrated at this fascinating museum, which features a rotating set of exhibits.

### 9. Palmer House Hilton

L4 17 E. Monroe St. chicagohilton.com

The original Palmer House, destroyed in the Chicago Fire, was replaced by this hotel, with frescoes and Tiffany lighting.

### 10. Daley Plaza

K4

Home to the county court headquarters, Daley Plaza is best known for its unnamed giant steel Picasso sculpture *(p76)* donated by the artist.

**Rock climbing structures at the Maggie Daley Park**

**Inside the spectacular multi-story Macy's**

## Shopping

### 1. Macy's

K4 111 N. State St.

Once Marshall Field's, Chicago's oldest and best-known department store, Macy's is famous for its elaborate Christmas displays, dazzling Tiffany dome, and an iconic clock. Established more than 100 years ago, it offers top clothing and homeware.

### 2. TJ Maxx

K4 11 N. State St.

This department store is a great place to find quality brands at cheap prices, with products for both adults and kids.

### 3. Block 37

K4 108 N. State St.

The Loop's answer to the malls of the Magnificent Mile, Block 37 features brands such as Sephora and Zara. Its food hall is great for lunch.

### 4. UNIQLO

K4 22 N. State St.

An outpost of the Japanese retailer, UNIQLO is best known for its casual-wear and accessories for all age groups.

### 5. Graham Crackers

L4 77 E. Madison St.

A treasure trove for fans of comics and graphic novels, this shop offers a vast selection of both new and historic editions, along with collectible action figures and toys.

### 6. Jewelers Center

K4 5 S. Wabash Ave. Sun

On the strip commonly known as "Jewelers Row," this 1912 Art Deco building contains over 180 jewelers. It is a good place to shop for gold, pearls, diamonds, and gems at relatively low prices.

### 7. Nordstrom Rack

K4 24 N. State St.

This charming little sister of the upscale and pricey Nordstrom draws bargain hunters with its high fashion, on sale at a fraction of the original prices.

### 8. Blick Art Materials

K4 16 W. Randolph St.

This two-story family-owned store offers a wide range of cards, stationery, and arty gifts in addition to its massive stock of fine art supplies.

### 9. Gallery 37 Store

L4 66 E. Randolph St.

Teenage artists involved in an arts training program create the incredible paintings, sculptures, and other artworks sold here. All proceeds from sales are reinvested into the program.

### 10. Iwan Ries and Co.

L4 19 S. Wabash Ave. Sun

Trading since 1857, this store sells a vast selection of cigars, pipes, and smoking accessories.

# Places to Eat

**PRICE CATEGORIES**

Price categories include a three-course meal for one, a glass of house wine, tax, and a 15–20 percent tip.

$ under $30 $$ $30–$75 $$$ over $75

### 1. The Berghoff

K4 17 W. Adams St.
theberghoff.com · $$

German-inspired fare, such as *brats*, and brews dominate the menu at this historic restaurant, serving Chicagoans since the 1890s.

### 2. The Gage

L4 24 S. Michigan Ave.
thegagechicago.com · $$$

This popular restaurant, located across from Millennium Park, offers a contemporary seasonal menu and an Irish-inspired concept, complete with Guinness on draft.

### 3. Au Cheval

J4 800 W. Randolph St.
auchevaldiner.com · $$

Brendan Sodikoff's upscale diner has a cult following, thanks to its excellent burgers and fried bologna sandwich – just be prepared for long lines.

### 4. Girl and the Goat

H4 809 W. Randolph St.
girlandthegoat.com · $$$

*Top Chef* winner Stephanie Izard helms this famous restaurant, known for its goat dishes and bold flavors. Reservations are advised, or arrive early.

### 5. Lou Mitchell's

J4 565 W. Jackson Blvd.
loumitchells.com D · $

Head to Lou's for a classic diner breakfast including to-die-for homemade skillet hashbrowns and double-yolk-eggs.

### 6. Petterino's

K4 150 Dearborn St.
petterinos.com · $$

This restaurant looks like a supper club with its jacketed waiters, but it operates with modern efficiency. Good pastas and chops are on the menu, and the bar is a popular post-curtain haunt for actors.

### 7. Atwood

K4 Staypineapple Chicago, 1 W. Washington St.
atwoodrestaurant.com · $$

Expect top-notch hotel dining, where creative American cuisine leans toward comfort food.

### 8. Cindy's

L4 12 S. Michigan Ave.
cindysrooftop.com · $$$

Crowds flock to Cindy's for the views. Its menu caters to a convivial crowd, with dishes like seafood platters.

### 9. Avec

J4 615 W. Randolph St.
avecrestaurant.com · $$

Known for its cozy dining room, Avec serves shareable Mediterranean bites and wines that pair perfectly.

### 10. Russian Tea Time

K4 77 E. Adams St.
russianteatime.com · $$

Founded by Ukrainian immigrants in 1993, this local institution serves up dishes such as borscht, *latkes* (potato pancakes), and *vareniki* (dumplings).

**Enjoying al fresco dining at Lou Mitchell's**

# NEAR NORTH

**History, culture, and commerce collide on Chicago's densely packed Near North side. This area is a pleasure to explore on foot, whether you are interested in shopping or fine art and architecture. The city's classiest shopping boulevard – the Magnificent Mile – bridges the posh 19th-century mansions of the lakeside Gold Coast (which has its own clutch of upscale boutiques) and the former industrial warehouses of River North, now mostly converted into art galleries. In addition to these, there are two local art museums and a burgeoning district of bars and restaurants.**

*For places to stay in this area, see p119*

**Art Deco Merchandise Mart on Wacker Drive**

## 1 Merchandise Mart

K3 222 W. Merchandise Mart Plaza themart.com

This massive two-square-block edifice houses Chicago's premier interior design trade showrooms. When completed in 1930, the four million-sq-ft (390,000-sq-m) building was the largest in the world. Today, it is second only to the Pentagon in size, and is one of the world's largest commercial buildings. The Chicago Architecture Center *(architecture.org)* offers a 45-minute guided tour, which is a great way to get to grips with this daunting building.

## 2 John Hancock Center

L2 875 N. Michigan Ave. Observatory: 9am–11pm daily 875northmichiganavenue.com

Architectural firm Skidmore, Owings & Merrill designed this 1970 landmark using the signature Xs on the facade as cross-braces to help the 1,100-ft (335-m) building withstand the winds coming off Lake Michigan. Soak up the view from the 94th-floor at 360 Chicago *(360chicago.com)*, home to the interactive TILT viewing experience, and the stylish Cloud Bar – both included with admission. Many say you get a better view from here than from the South Side's Sears Tower.

## 3 The Magnificent Mile

Whether you're a serial shopper or not, this store-lined strip *(p40)* warrants a visit if only to get a feel for the commercial pulse that seems to keep Chicago humming.

## 4 Museum of Contemporary Art Chicago (MCA)

L2 220 E. Chicago Ave. 10am–9pm Tue, 10am–5pm Wed–Sun mcachicago.org

One of the country's largest collections of contemporary art, the MCA has over 2,500 objects, from paintings and sculptures to photography and video installations. In summer, the sculpture garden and performance art on the front lawn enhance the experience.

## 5 Gold Coast Area

K1

Chicago has a number of upscale neighborhoods, but none more historic and prestigious than the Gold Coast. Its streets are lined with 19th-century mansions interspersed with early 20th-century apartment buildings. There are no fewer than 300 designated historic landmarks in the Astor Street District alone, including buildings by Stanford White (such as 20 E. Burton Place), and Charnley House *(1365 N. Astor Street)*, designed by Louis Sullivan.

**Grand interior of Fourth Presbyterian Church**

## 6 Fourth Presbyterian Church

L2 126 E. Chestnut St.
10am–2pm Mon–Fri & Sun
fourthchurch.org

The first Fourth Presbyterian church, dedicated in 1871, celebrated its first sermon just hours before it was incinerated in the Great Fire. Rebuilt in 1914, the church offers a peaceful respite from the Magnificent Mile. Designed by Ralph Adams Cram, one of the architects behind New York's Cathedral of St. John the Divine, this church has a cathedral-like interior, with a splendid stained-glass west window. Free concerts take place on Fridays at noon.

## 7 Chicago Water Works and Pumping Station

L2 163 E. Pearson St. and 806 N. Michigan Ave.

When the Great Fire of 1871 swept north, only two structures survived: the 1869 Water Tower and its neighboring Pumping Station. Designed by William W. Boyington, the Gothic Revival waterworks facility was modeled after a medieval castle and built to resolve Chicago's water supply challenges. Today, it houses the Lookingglass Theatre *(p63)*. The fountain and seating area make it a focal point for street life.

## 8 Tribune Tower

L3 435 N. Michigan Ave.

Topped by flying buttresses, this Gothic-style building was completed in 1925. Its faux-historic design had won a competition organized by Colonel Robert McCormick, publisher of the *Chicago Tribune*, the newspaper whose offices occupied the building until 2018. The building's extravagant three-story arched entrance is adorned with carvings of figures from Aesop's fables. Look closely at the facade, which is embedded with over 120 stones collected by correspondents from famed sights. There's a rock hailing from each of the 50 states in the US, as well as fragments from international monuments such as Greece's Parthenon, India's Taj Mahal, and the Great Wall of China.

## 9 Newberry Library

K2 60 W. Walton St.
10am–7pm Tue–Thu, 10am–5pm Fri & Sat newberry.org

Founded in 1887 by wealthy Chicago businessman Walter L. Newberry, this research library is housed in a Romanesque-style granite building designed by architect Henry Ives Cob.

**River North Gallery District along the Chicago River**

It is stocked with rare books, maps, manuscripts, and music, and has research centers devoted to the history of cartography, Indigenous studies, the Renaissance, and American history and culture. It also offers seminars on everything from Greek literature to genealogy research. The public can access the collections by applying for a reader's card, free of charge.

## 10 River North Gallery District

K3

Bounded by Merchandise Mart to the south, Chicago Avenue to the north, Orleans Avenue to the west, and Dearborn Street to the east, River North is said to be the most concentrated art hub in the US outside of Manhattan. This vibrant district is packed with galleries, most of which are housed in 19th-century converted brick warehouses lining the "L" brown line. Huron and Superior streets are especially worth a visit. For up-to-date information on the galleries in the area, check out Chicago Gallery News *(chicagogallerynews.com)*.

### A DAY IN THE NEAR NORTH

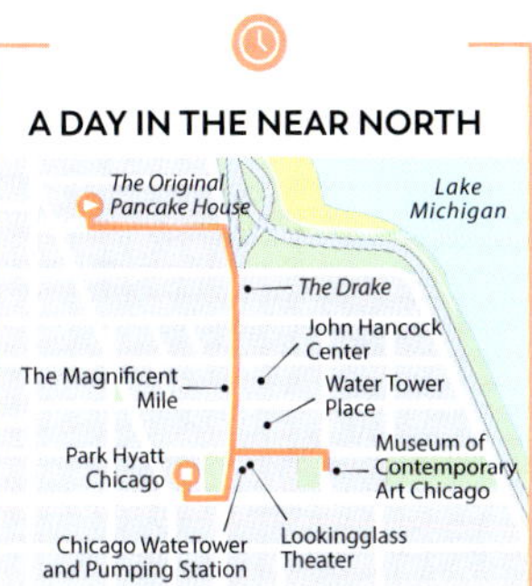


#### Morning

Line up early for a fortifying stack at **The Original Pancake House** *(22 E. Bellevue Pl; ophchicago land.com)*. Afterward, stroll south on Rush Street to Oak Street. Take a left and walk the most exclusive shopping block in the city, where you can pop into stores such as Tory Burch, Loro Piana, and more. Once you hit Michigan Avenue, it's a short jaunt to the **John Hancock Center** *(p83)* for superb views. Back on terra firma, cross the street to the **Chicago Water Tower and Pumping Station** for a look at a piece of the city's history. Lovers of modern art should cross Michigan again and head to the **Museum of Contemporary Art Chicago** *(p83)*. For lunch, head to the food court on the second level of the mall in **Water Tower Place** *(p34)*.

#### Afternoon

After lunch, you can shop at Chicago's first ever vertical mall, and then shop some more – and sightsee – along **The Magnificent Mile** *(p40)*. If you've worked up an appetite, stroll over to **The Drake** hotel *(p52)* for high tea, which is served until 4:30pm. Catch a show at the **Lookingglass Theater** housed in the **Chicago Water Tower and Pumping Station**. Then head to chic NoMI *(p87)* in the **Park Hyatt Chicago** for dinner and drinks with panoramic views of downtown Chicago.

# Shopping

**Entrance to the popular American Girl Place**

### 1. Patagonia

L2 48 E. Walton St.
patagonia.com
Gear up for adventures at this outdoors outfitter, known for its cold weather staples such as fleece jumpers and down coats.

### 2. Nike

L2 669 N. Michigan Ave.
nike.com/retail/s/nike-chicago
The Chicago flagship of this iconic sports brand is a massive bi-level space with eye-catching displays of sports gear and athleisure clothing.

### 3. American Girl Place

L2 Water Tower Place, 835 N. Michigan Ave. americangirl.com
This store, the only retail outlet for the American Girl doll line, is frequented by parents of children aged 4 to 12.

### 4. Ikram

L2 15 E. Huron St. ikram.com
Launched by a former Ultimo buyer, Ikram features high-end women's fashion sold at top dollar.

### 5. Polo Ralph Lauren

L2 750 N. Michigan Ave.
ralphlauren.global
This massive, four-storied shop is a den devoted to everything Ralph Lauren. With numerous pictures of horses and hounds throughout, it is the biggest Ralph Lauren store in the world.

### 6. Anthropologie

K2 111 E. Chicago Ave.
anthropologie.com
Alternative women's apparel and stylish housewares gathered from around the world sell briskly at this large, loft-like store.

### 7. P.O.S.H.

K3 613 N. State St.
poshchicago.com
Recalling the days of steamships and grand hotels, this store uses old-fashioned suitcases and steamer trunks to lovingly display vintage china and silverware engraved with hotel and ship logos.

### 8. Paper Source

J2 232 W. Chicago Ave.
papersource.com
This arty River North shop is part art supply store, part stationer. Its creative selection includes handmade stationery, cloth-covered sketchbooks, and novel desktop accessories.

### 9. Neiman Marcus

L2 737 N Michigan Ave.
neimanmarcus.com
This is a massive branch of the Texas-based department store, known for its designer cosmetics and fashion brands.

### 10. Bloomingdale's

L2 900 N. Michigan Ave.
bloomingdales.com
An outpost of New York's posh department store that features house designer boutiques and a well-stocked shoe department.

## Places to Eat

### 1. Frontera Grill

K3 445 N. Clark St. Mon
fronteragrill.com · $$

Chef Rick Bayless' regional Mexican cuisine warrants the two-margarita waits that inevitably face diners at Frontera Grill.

**PRICE CATEGORIES**

Price categories include a three-course meal for one, a glass of house wine, tax, and a 15–20 percent tip.

$ under $30 $$ $30–$75 $$$ over $75

### 2. NoMI

L2 800 N. Michigan Ave.
nomichicago.com · $$$

On the seventh floor of the Park Hyatt Chicago, overlooking the landmark Water Tower, NoMI is a refined restaurant with a menu featuring sushi and steak.

### 3. Billy Goat Tavern

L3 Lower 430 N. Michigan Ave. billygoattavern.com · $

This legendary dive bar has been serving cold beer, classic "cheezborgers," and hot dogs at this location since 1964. Stop by to hear the legendary tale of "the curse of the Billy Goat."

### 4. RL

L2 115 E. Chicago Ave.
ralphlauren.com/global-rl-chicago · $$$

This in-store steakhouse and power-spot is furnished in upper-crust style by the Ralph Lauren Home shop. The menu is inspired by classic American food.

**Elegant interior of NoMI at Park Hyatt**

### 5. The Purple Pig

L3 444 N. Michigan Ave.
thepurplepigchicago.com · $$

Suitable for both happy hour spreads and coursed meals, this cozy venue is always buzzing with its loyal patrons.

### 6. Gene and Georgetti

J3 500 N. Franklin St.
geneandgeorgetti.com · $$$

White tablecloths, martinis, and classic red sauce are the hallmarks at this popular steakhouse.

### 7. Ambassador Room

L2 1301 N. State Pkwy. thechicagohotelcollection.com · $$$

At this lounge, formerly known as the Pump Room, diners can enjoy a classic continental menu and live jazz performances.

### 8. Mr. Beef

J2 666 N. Orleans St.
theoriginalmrbeef.com · $

Known for its beef sandwiches, this restaurant served as the inspiration for the TV show *The Bear*.

### 9. Gibson's Steakhouse

L2 1028 N. Rush St.
gibsonssteakhouse.com · $$$

A favorite with locals and visitors alike, Gibson's offers a classic Chicago steakhouse experience.

### 10. Pizzeria Uno

L3 29 E. Ohio St.
pizzeriaunodue.com · $$

Famous for its deep-dish pizza, this spot is a must-visit for anyone in search of Chicago-style pizza.

# NORTHSIDE

**Encompassing parts of Old Town, Lincoln Park, Lakeview, and Wrigleyville, Chicago's Northside has upscale restaurants and chi-chi boutiques galore, as well as some of the city's best bars and one of its most progressive theater companies, Steppenwolf. Older buildings have been transformed into beautiful condominiums with stylish new apartments. In baseball season, nearby Wrigley Field fans bolster the lively Wrigleyville atmosphere by swarming the surrounding streets and bars. The vibrant LGBTQ+ hub of Northalsted is also in this area, while running along Northside's eastern border is the incredible lakefront.**

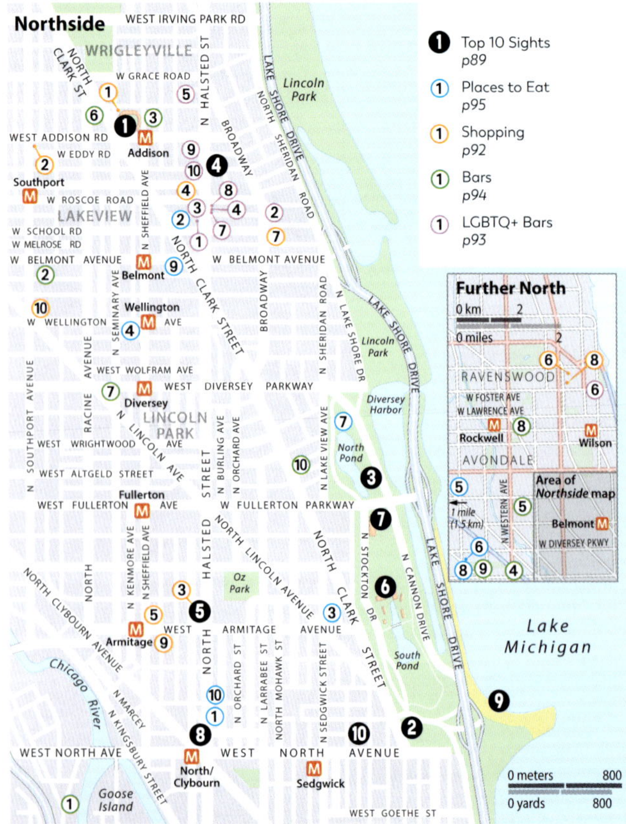


*For places to stay in this area, see p120*

**Wrigley Field, during a Chicago Cubs game**

## 1 Wrigley Field

D1 1060 W. Addison St. mlb.com/cubs

Built in 1914, this is the US's oldest National League baseball park. The home team, the Chicago Cubs, hadn't won a World Series championship since 1908 (before the field even existed), but that changed in 2016, breaking the fabled "Curse of the Billy Goat." From March to September, spend an afternoon at this iconic stadium, cheering on the "Cubbies" inside the signature ivy-covered walls – a quintessential Chicago experience.

## 2 Chicago History Museum

F4 1601 N. Clark St. 9:30am–4:30pm Tue–Sat, noon–5pm Sun chicagohistory.org

Focusing on Illinois and Chicago history since settler days, this museum was established in 1856 by the Chicago Historical Society, and is the city's oldest cultural institution. One of the society's first donors bequeathed his collection of Lincoln memorabilia to the museum; the former president's deathbed is one of the items displayed here. Visitors can climb aboard the Pioneer locomotive and explore the many exhibits and photography displays dedicated to historic events such as the World's Columbian Exposition *(p33)* and the Great Chicago Fire *(p9)*. There is also a vast collection of uniforms here, which range from the mid-18th century military outfits to present-day sports jerseys, belonging to famous figures including George Washington and Michael Jordan.

## 3 Peggy Notebaert Nature Museum

F3 2430 N. Cannon Dr. 10am–4pm daily naturemuseum.org

This museum's sloping, beige exterior was inspired by the sand dunes that once occupied its site. Inside are numerous engrossing interactive exhibits, the highlight being the walk-through "Butterfly Haven."

## 4 Northalsted

E1–E2 northalsted.com

Primarily located along North Halsted Street, and much of Broadway, Northalsted stretches from Belmont Avenue to Grace Street and along Clark Street from Belmont to Addison avenues. Once a declining industrial district, this neighborhood, formerly known as Boystown, has transformed into a hub for artisan retailers, trendy galleries, and popular nightclubs. Although it has long been known as a gay-friendly neighborhood, a concerted effort has been made to make the area more inclusive of other LGBTQ+ communities.

**Rainbow pylons in Northalsted**

## 5 Armitage/Halsted Shopping District

**E4**

Located in the Lincoln Park neighborhood, this area of unique boutiques is a boon for fashionistas. Dozens of shops here sell everything from sophisticated evening wear to high-end accessories. Many of the stores occupy renovated Victorian town homes, which are set along pretty, tree-lined streets.

## 6 Lincoln Park Zoo

**F3 2001 N. Clark St. Grounds: 7am–6pm daily; buildings: Apr–Oct: 8am–5pm daily (to 7pm Sat, Sun & hols); Nov–Mar: 10am–4:30pm daily lpzoo.org**

Established in 1868 with just a pair of swans, the beloved Lincoln Park Zoo has become an important part of the Northside community. Wildlife such as tropical birds, big cats, primates, and reptiles thrive here in enclosures that recreate the various species' natural habitats. The activity-oriented Endangered Species Carousel and Farm-in-the-Zoo are must-sees for children.

## 7 Lincoln Park Conservatory

**F3 2391 N. Stockton Dr. 10am–5pm Wed–Sun lincolnparkconservancy.org**

Take a free trip to the tropics at this spacious conservatory, just next to Lincoln Park Zoo. Opened in 1893, the glass structure is a year-round, 80° F (40° C) sanctuary from Chicago's bustle, and offers a welcome respite from the city's long winters. Paths meander past lush palms, flourishing ferns, and exquisite 100-year-old orchids. Avoid the crowds by coming on a weekday when, unless a seasonal show is taking place, it's a quiet space, with trickling water as the only background sound.

## 8 Steppenwolf Theater Co.

**E4 1650 N. Halsted St. steppenwolf.org**

Founded in 1974 in a church basement, this theater company grew quickly to include a corps of actors who would become famous on stage and screen, including John Malkovich and Gary Sinise. Now based in a modern complex with two full stages and the smaller Garage Theater, Steppenwolf has sent many hits to New York's Broadway over the years.

## 9 North Avenue Beach

**F4 Lakeshore Dr. and North Ave. Dawn–dusk daily**

When summer graces Chicago with its presence, locals of all ages and nationalities converge on this short,

**Jogging path along the North Avenue Beach**

but inviting beach. Running along its edge is the lakefront path, where cyclists, in-line skaters, runners, and walkers stream by. Swimming is permitted from Memorial Day to Labor Day, when lifeguards are on duty. Confident folks strut their stuff at the outdoor gym, while the sand volleyball courts allow the energetic to let off steam. For a relaxing drink with a view of the activities below, the rooftop bar of the steamship-shaped beach house is an ideal spot.

## 10 Second City

F4 1616 N. Wells St.
secondcity.com

It's hard to overstate the influence that Second City has had on comedy in America since it opened it doors at North Wells Street in 1959. The home of improvisational comedy, Second City has been the starting point for an army of talent from John Belushi, Dan Aykroyd, and Bill Murray to Tina Fey and Stephen Colbert. On two stages at its headquarters in Old Town, Second City offers full-length shows (another venue, UP Comedy Club on West North Avenue, is reserved for stand-up comedy). Seating for all shows is done on a first come first served basis, but all seats have good views.

**Lush gardens at the Lincoln Park Conservatory**

## EXPLORING NORTHSIDE

### Morning

Fuel up for the day at one of Lincoln Park's favorite breakfast joints, **The Brunchery** *(2552 N. Clark St.)*, where a wonderfully fluffy French toast is served. Afterwards, take a stroll east down Wrightwood Avenue and keep walking until you come to the **Lincoln Park Zoo**, where you can ride on the wild side on the African Safari motion simulator. Then, head for a lunch with a view at **Café Brauer** *(2021 N. Stockton Dr.)*, built in 1908 by Prairie School architect Dwight Perkins.

### Afternoon

During warm weather, head to the lakefront along Fullerton Avenue where you can stroll, rent bikes, sunbathe, or even brave the chilly Lake Michigan waters. In colder months, catch a bus (nos. 22 or 151) and visit the **Chicago History Museum** *(p89)*, or cycle for ten minutes to the **Armitage/ Halsted Shopping District** for some retail therapy. This part of town has excellent restaurants: hop the "L" four stops or cycle to **Mia Francesca** *(p95)*, an Italian trattoria where the pasta dishes are big enough for two, and there's a great wine list. Round off your day with a visit to **Kingston Mines** *(kingstonmines.com)* – just a 20-minute walk away – to hear some of the city's blues musicians.

# Shopping

### 1. Chicago Cubs Team Store

B1 3637 N. Clark St.,Wrigley Field

Located right next to the famous baseball stadium *(p89)*, the official Cubs store is open daily, including on game days. It offers a wide array of Cubs merchandise and jerseys, alongside quirky city souvenirs.

### 2. Paper Source

D1 3543 N. Southport Ave.

Originally an artists' supply store, Paper Source now concentrates on stationery and paper goods, ranging from origami papers and handmade gift-wrap sheets to stylish notecards and greeting cards. A craft area hosts workshops in card making.

### 3. Lori's Shoes

E4 824 W. Armitage Ave.

Devoted shoe hounds flock to this store for its hot styles and reduced prices. The floors and walls are stacked high with boxes for handy self-serve and try-on access.

### 4. Beatnix

E2 3400 N. Halsted St.

This store offers the best supply of costumes and vintage gear in the city, including wigs, distinctive mod jewelry, and make-up.

**Wide range of stationery on display at Paper Source**

### 5. Art Effect

E4 934 W. Armitage Ave.

An institution on the trendy Armitage Avenue since 1984, this eclectic boutique offers a little bit of everything, from offbeat fashion, accessories, and statement jewelry to retro toys for kids and unusual homewares.

### 6. Andersonville Galleria

B3 5247 N. Clark St.

Artists, jewelers, fashion designers, knitters, and more maintain booths at Andersonville Galleria, a creative co-op. You could easily spend a few hours wandering around the three-story maze.

### 7. Unabridged Bookstore

E2 3521 N. Broadway

Acclaimed for its large LGBTQ+ section, this award-winning bookstore in Northalsted also has an excellent collection of children's books and Spanish-language titles.

### 8. Scout Chicago

B3 5221 N. Clark St.

An antique shop with a funky flare for mid-century modern and industrial one-offs, Scout always stocks surprises such as old gym lockers, in cramped, but intriguing quarters.

### 9. Kiehl's

E4 907 W. Armitage Ave.

773-665-2515

Established in New York in 1851, this classic apothecary has helpful staff in white lab coats who walk customers through an extensive line of skincare and wellness products.

### 10. Three Avenues Bookstore

D2 3009 N. Southport Ave.

Opened by a local couple in 2022, this indie bookstore features an artfully curated selection and a knowledgeable staff. It also hosts literary events regularly.

Popular Kit Kat Lounge and Supper Club

## LGBTQ+ Bars

### 1. Scarlet Bar

E2 3320 N. Halsted St.

This big party bar has fun themed events and happy hours every night from Thursday to Sunday. Note, it only accepts credit and debit cards.

### 2. The Closet

E2 3325 N. Broadway

This dance club attracts a mostly lesbian crowd, but gay men and straight couples also groove to R&B, rap, dance, and diva videos.

### 3. Roscoe's Tavern

E2 3356 N. Halsted St.

A young, preppy set packs this neighborhood bar for its antique decor, cozy fireplace, cheesy dance tunes, and, in summer, beer garden.

### 4. Sidetrack

E2 3349 N. Halsted St.

Featuring four rooms, this vast bar has more than two dozen video monitors that highlight a different theme (such as show tunes or 1980s music) every night.

### 5. Kit Kat Lounge and Supper Club

E2 3700 N. Halsted St.

D daily, Sun brunch

Martinis come in 52 flavors at this chic spot, where drag queens show their lip-syncing talent.

### 6. Big Chicks

B3 5024 N. Sheridan Rd.

A local LGBTQ+ favorite, and one of Chicago's most welcoming bars, Big Chick's hosts popular trivia nights and Bear Den nights.

### 7. Splash Chicago

E2 3339 N. Halsted St.

This edgy and friendly gay bar attracts a fun and varied crowd every night. After midnight, the dance floor rocks with a stellar sound system and dazzling light show.

### 8. Progress Bar

E2 3359 N. Halsted St.

Sit back and sip on must-try martinis while people-watching Northalsted folks through wall-to-wall windows at this sleek bar.

### 9. Elixir

E2 3452 N. Halsted St.

This dark little cocktail den is a nice antidote to the louder options down the street.

### 10. Hydrate

E2 3458 N. Halsted St.

Hydrate features a bar in front with roll-up garage-style doors, and a dance floor out back that cranks into the early hours. A drag queen show "Beautie and Beaus" takes place on Saturday nights.

# Bars

### 1. Goose Island Salt Shed Pub

G1 11221 W. Blackhawk St.

Chicago's pioneering microbrewery is a local favorite, offering a diverse range of beers. Enjoy lovely outdoor seating along the Chicago River, adjacent to the Salt Shed live venue.

### 2. Schubas Tavern and Tied House

D1 3159 N. Southport Ave.

Twenty-somethings dress down for beer, live music, and a hip restaurant that packs in crowds, especially on the patio during warm-weather weekends.

### 3. The Tin Lizzie

E3 2483 N. Clark St.

A sports bar and dance club, Tin Lizzie is packed wall-to-wall with twenty- to thirty-somethings most weekends.

### 4. Map Room

B4 1949 N. Hoyne St.

With an impressive menu of global beers, Map Room draws an eclectic crowd to peruse its stacks of old *National Geographic* magazines.

### 5. Village Tap

D1 2055 W. Roscoe St.

Popular for its back patio, this bar in laid-back Roscoe village offers a strong selection of tap beers and pub food.

**Enjoying a drink at the bar at Schubas Tavern**

### 6. GMan Tavern

D1 3740 N. Clark St.

A Wrigleyville stalwart, GMan is not a sports bar despite being in the home of the Chicago Cubs. It has a range of beers and a few pool tables.

### 7. Delilah's

D2 2771 N. Lincoln Ave.

Called one of "the great whiskey bars in the world" by *Whiskey Magazine*, Delilah's has been a neighborhood watering hole for years. It has over 1,000 types of spirits on offer, not to mention the many beers on tap.

### 8. Lincoln Square Taproom

B3 4721 N. Lincoln Ave.

In the historically German district of Lincoln Square, this spot channels old-world *gemuetlichkeit*, or warmth, with flower-box-trimmed front windows and German beer on tap.

### 9. The Whistler

B4 2421 N. Milwaukee Ave.

A low-key cocktail bar, the Whistler buzzes with DJ sets and live jazz during the week, and fun dance parties on weekends.

### 10. Murphy's Bleachers

E1 3655 N. Sheffield Ave.

Located near the Wrigley Field *(p89)*, Murphy's Bleachers is a long-standing tavern with a loyal following of Cubs fanatics as well as fair-weather drinkers.

# Places to Eat

**PRICE CATEGORIES**

Price categories include a three-course meal for one, a glass of house wine, tax, and a 15–20 percent tip.

$ under $30 $$ $30–$75 $$$ over $75

### 1. Alinea

E4 1723 N. Halsted St.
alinearestaurant.com · $$$

This high-end, fine-dining restaurant serves delicious unique food pairings in a stylish setting. Sample its famed New American tasting menus.

### 2. Mia Francesca

F4 3311 N. Clark St. L
miafrancesca.com · $$

The wait for the generous portions of flavorful pastas, seafood, and chicken at this lively spot is worth it.

### 3. Geja's Café

E4 340 W. Armitage Ave.
Mon & Tue gejascafe.com · $$$

Opened in 1965, this romantic café offers the ultimate fondue experience in a delightful setting. Choose cheese or hot oil, or just opt for the decadent chocolate fondue.

### 4. Fish Bar

E2 2956 N. Sheffield 773-681-8177 11:30am–10pm daily (to midnight Fri & Sat) · $

This small restaurant serves the best fish in the city – everything from salmon, oysters, and tilapia to classic fish and chips.

### 5. Smoque

A4 3800 N. Pulaski Rd.
Mon smoquebbq.com · $

Ranked one of the best BBQ places in the US, Smoque attracts serious meat lovers with its smoker grills churning out BBQ ribs, brisket, and pulled pork in St. Louis and Memphis style.

**Wood-paneled dining room at North Pond**

### 6. Longman and Eagle

B4 2657 N. Kedzie Ave.
longmanandeagle.com · $$

This trendy gastropub takes its farm-fresh fare seriously but has a casual atmosphere in its two packed rooms.

### 7. North Pond

F3 2610 N. Cannon Dr.
L daily (except Sun brunch)
northpondrestaurant.com · $$$

A former "warming house" for skaters, this pond-side restaurant serves up American gourmet cuisine.

### 8. Lula Café

B4 2537 N. Kedzie Ave.
Thu–Sun lulacafe.com · $$

An eclectic café in Logan Square, Lula champions local and organic ingredients in its farm-to-table meals, from morning through late night.

### 9. Ann Sather

E2 909 W. Belmont Ave.
annsather.com · $

Known for its delicious breakfasts, this Swedish restaurant also serves lunchtime specialties.

### 10. Boka

E4 1729 N. Halsted St.
L bokachicago.com · $$

The Michelin-starred Boka offers elegant, seasonally informed food in a series of rooms.

# SOUTH LOOP

**Just south of the business-centric Loop, this multicultural area is home to an array of upscale addresses and historical neighborhoods, including Chinatown. In the 19th century, wealthy residents, such as George Pullman and Marshall Field, lived alongside the burgeoning railroad industry. However, both the wealthy residents and local businesses deserted the loop in the 20th century. Only in the 1980s did the city make a concerted effort to revitalize the area. Thanks to this, the South Loop today has many "must-sees," but the jewel in the crown is the Museum Campus: here, the Field Museum, Shedd Aquarium, and Adler Planetarium celebrate the wonders of the earth, sea, and sky respectively. The highway that once separated the Field from its neighbors has been replaced by an inviting green campus, where cyclists and skaters join museum-goers on the plant-bordered paths in fair weather.**

## 1 Prairie Avenue District

C5

Of the wealthy enclaves both north and south of the Chicago River that emerged following the Great Fire of 1871, Prairie Avenue was the most fashionable and ritziest. Only a few of the old mansions remain today, of which two are open to the public: the Romanesque-Revival Glessner House *(1800 S. Prairie Ave.)*, constructed in 1887, and Chicago's oldest building, Clarke House *(1827 S. Indiana Ave.)*, built in 1836. The houses are accessible through guided tours *(312-326-1480)* only from July to September.

## 2 Blues Heaven Foundation

C5 2120 S. Michigan Ave.
For tours, check website
bluesheaven.com

Located in the former studios of Chess Records, where blues greats from Muddy Waters to Willie Dixon once recorded, Blues Heaven has records, photos, and costumes dedicated to Chicago's blues style and its artists. The original label's music plays throughout and live performances are also held. Note, advance bookings are mandatory for entry.

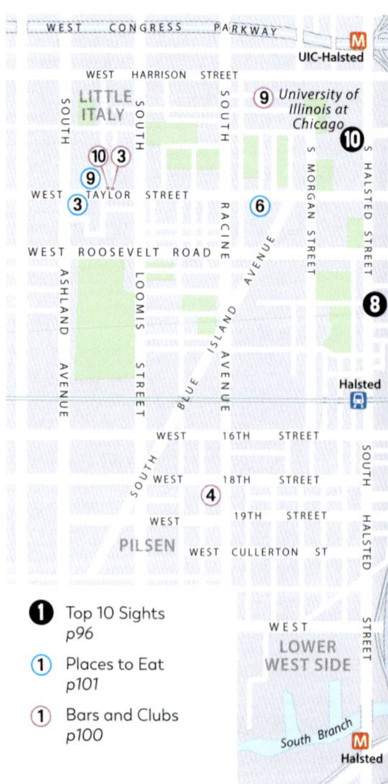

## 3 Shedd Aquarium

One of the three institutions to occupy the Museum Campus, the Shedd *(p36)* is one of the oldest and most visited public aquariums in the world. Nearly 32,000 saltwater and freshwater animals live here. Dive in to discover the many treasures of the aquatic world on show.

## 4 Adler Planetarium

**M6 1300 S. Lake Shore Dr.**
**9am–4pm daily (to 10pm Wed)**
**adlerplanetarium.org**

The Western Hemisphere's first planetarium, the Adler is the Museum Campus's star attraction. It chronicles more than 1,000 years of astronomical discoveries. Don't miss the Grainger Sky Theater show, which is projected on the 68-ft (21-m) dome of the historic Zeiss planetarium.

**Indigenous artifacts at the Field Museum**

## 5 Field Museum

The last of three Museum Campus sights, the Field Museum *(p28)* is one of the largest natural history museums in the world. It features a collection of more than 40 million fascinating natural history and anthropological artifacts from around the world.

***For places to stay in this area, see p121***

**Relaxing on a bench at Northerly Island**

## 6 Northerly Island

**M6 1521 S. Linn White Dr. 6am–11pm daily chicagoparkdistrict.com**

The city's premier lakefront park, Northerly Island was envisioned by city planner Daniel H. Burnham as part of his lakefront plan. Located south of the Adler Planetarium, this lovely green space features lush gardens with native flora and walking trails. It also includes an outdoor concert stage.

## 7 Museum of Contemporary Photography

**L5 600 S. Michigan Ave. 10am–5pm Mon–Sat (to 8pm Thu) mocp.org**

Run by and located in Columbia College Chicago, this museum is one of a kind in the Midwest. It exhibits the portfolios of international modern artists, with shows tending toward the experimental, rather than the traditional documentary. Changing exhibitions also present a mix of local talents and well-established ones, such as Gary Winogrand and William Eggleston. Frequent gallery talks give curators and artists the chance to discuss the shows with museum-goers.

## 8 Maxwell Street Market

**J6 May–Oct: 10am–3pm on select days, check website chicago.gov**

Both 19th-century European migrants and 20th-century Black settlers fleeing the Deep South of America got their entrepreneurial start here selling from pushcarts around Maxwell Street. In 1994 the market was relocated to make way for the new University of Illinois at Chicago and, while a shadow of its former self, it still makes for a vibrant Sunday morning. Among the Mexican housewares and secondhand tools for sale, the occasional treasure (such as a vintage coat) shows up. Another reason to visit is to try the homemade tacos from the Mexican food stalls that line the street between South Halsted Street and South Union Avenue.

## 9 Chinatown

**B5**

Crowned by the landmark Chinatown Gate spanning Wentworth Avenue and Cermak Road, Chicago's Chinatown isn't very large – running roughly eight blocks – but it is colorful. Home to the city's oldest Asian community, Chinatown was founded in the 19th century by transcontinental railroad workers fleeing West Coast prejudice.

**Colorful signage in Chinatown**

Cantonese and Mandarin are still spoken far more widely here than English. Stroll along Wentworth to admire the ornate On Leong Tong Building, buy fresh almond cookies from Chinese bakeries, peruse the many herbal shops, or dine in one of the numerous local restaurants.

## 10 Jane Addams Hull-House

**H5 800 S. Halsted St. 10am–4:50pm Tue–Fri, 10am–3pm Sat hullhousemuseum.org**

Founded in the late 19th century by social reformer Jane Addams, Hull-House was a settlement house for European immigrants who came to Chicago to seek work in the rail and stockyards. The house also served as a welfare center for the immigrant working-class with facilities such as day care, employment counseling, and vocational training, alongside cultural programs like music and theater. Today, Hull-House is a prestigious museum and research center. Visitors can see Addams' former office, furniture, and artworks here. The museum's temporary exhibits trace the history of the house and explore the significant contributions of its residents. There's also a small library with books on local history and reform movements.

### EXPLORING SOUTH LOOP

#### Morning

Start by getting a coffee and cinnamon roll French toast at **Yolk** *(1120 S. Michigan Ave.; eatyolk.com)*. From there, walk through **Grant Park** *(p23)* to the **Museum Campus**. Here you can explore the **Field Museum** *(p28)*, **Adler Planetarium**, and **Shedd Aquarium** *(p36)*. If you plan to visit other museums, it makes sense to purchase a CityPass *(p36)*. If you opt to see the highlights of each, head to the Shedd Aquarium's Soundings Café for good food and great views of the lake.

#### Afternoon

Take a leisurely stroll from Adler Planetarium, heading south to Northerly Island for gorgeous skyline views. Walk back to Shedd Aquarium and then to the pedestrian bridge on 18th Street to get to the **Prairie Avenue District** *(p96)*. Here you can explore the historic streets and maybe even catch a tour of the **Glessner House** *(glessnerhouse.org)*. In the evening, head over to **Wabash Avenue** for an early supper a trendy restaurant on what is now a burgeoning strip. A popular spot is **Lowcountry South Loop** *(1132 S. Wabush Ave; lowcountrychicago.com)*, known for its Southern-style seafood and Cajun cuisine. After dinner, go on to **Buddy Guy's Legends** *(p100)* and hear the blues.

**Photos and memorabilia at Buddy Guy's Legends**

# Bars and Clubs

**1. Reggies**
K6 2105 S. State St.
reggieslive.com
This rock venue and grill-pub offers nightly musical entertainment and good bar fare.

**2. M Lounge**
K6 1520 S. Wabash Ave.
mloungechicago.com
Settle into cozy couches while enjoying a mix of traditional and modern jazz at M Lounge. Drop by on Thursdays for live music and karaoke.

**3. Vintage Bar**
G6 1449 W. Taylor St.
vintageontaylor.com
The mahogany bar and classic cocktails at Vintage Bar will take you back to Old Chicago. A range of pizzas and homemade donuts are on the menu.

**4. Punch House**
B5 1227 W. 18th St.
punchhousechicago.com
Hidden in the basement of Thalia Hall, Punch House looks like a swinging 1970s recreation room. Potent punches are the specialty of the house.

**5. Buddy Guy's Legends**
L5 700 S. Wabash Ave.
buddyguy.com
Ninety-year-old bluesman Buddy Guy runs and occasionally performs at this Chicago institution.

**6. Jazz Showcase**
K5 806 S. Plymouth Ct.
jazzshowcase.com
Since 1947, this has been Chicago's premiere jazz showroom, hosting the greats past and present. Sunday afternoon shows are family friendly.

**7. Kasey's Tavern**
K5 701 S. Dearborn Ave.
kaseystavern.com
A local favorite, Kasey's has been serving Printer's Row regulars since the early 1970s – though the historic pub dates back to the early 20th century.

**8. Duneyrr Wine and Beer Co**
B5 2337 S. Michigan Ave.
duneyrr.com
This local craft brewery draws inspiration from Belgian and Nordic ales. It also produces cider and botanical aperitifs, and features beers from Moderne Dune.

**9. Tufano's Vernon Park Tap**
H5 1073 W. Vernon Park Pl. Mon
This popular bar has legions of local and celebrity fans who pile in for house wine and generous, inexpensive pastas.

**10. Hawkeye's Bar and Grill**
G6 1458 W. Taylor St.
hawkeyeschicago.com
Try this sports bar for beer-fueled camaraderie and a slice of Chicago fan zeal. It also serves decent meals, including burgers, wings, and nachos.

# Places to Eat

### 1. Eleven City Diner

L6 1112 S. Wabash Ave.
elevencitydiner.com D · $

Enjoy deli-diner fare, featuring sandwiches, omelets, and pastries from the all-day breakfast menu. Try the old-fashioned fountain drinks, including classic egg cream.

### 2. The Chicago Firehouse Restaurant

L6 1401 S. Michigan Ave.
chicagofirehouse.com · $$$

Steaks and seafood are the staple in this former firehouse turned diner. Don't miss the hearty lobster bisque.

### 3. Pompei

G6 1531 W. Taylor St.
pompeiusa.com · $

This Little Italy lunch spot showcases a dozen delicious by-the-slice pizzas. Hot sandwiches and stuffed pastas round out the offerings.

### 4. Chiu Quon Bakery and Dim Sum

B5 2253 S. Wentworth Ave.
cqbakery.com · $

This Chinatown favorite prides itself on being the oldest Chinese bakery in Chicago. Featured on the hit show *The Bear*, it is best known for its BBQ pork buns, dumplings (and dim sum), and egg custard tarts.

**The outside of the French bistro, Chez Joel**

**PRICE CATEGORIES**

Price categories include a three-course meal for one, a glass of house wine, tax, and a 15–20 percent tip.

**$** under $30 **$$** $30–$75 **$$$** over $75

### 5. Cafécito

H6 26 E. Ida B. Wells Dr.
iheartcafecito.com · $

Cuban-style paninis, café con leche, and *batidos* (milkshakes) are the draw at this lively café.

### 6. Chez Joel

H6 1119 W. Taylor St. Sun
chezjoelbistro.com · $$$

A unique French bistro in the heart of Little Italy charms fans with its sunny decor and fine classics.

### 7. Moody Tongue

H6 2515 S. Wabash Ave.
moodytongue.com · $$$

A casual tasting room and a fine dining restaurant are housed under one roof here, with Michelin-starred chefs pairing bites with beer.

### 8. Phoenix

A6 2131 S. Archer Ave.
312-328-0848 · $

Phoenix attracts dim sum diners from near and far. Visit early on weekends or prepare for long waits.

### 9. Rosebud Cafe

G6 1500 W. Taylor St.
rosebudrestaurants.com · $$

The Italian cooking at Rosebud's, located in Little Italy, isn't daring but its convivial vibe is hard to resist.

### 10. Mercat a la Planxa

L5 638 S. Michigan Ave.
mercatchicago.com · $$

The lively Mercat a la Planxa specializes in tapas such as bacon-wrapped dates and juicy lamb chops.

# FAR SOUTH

**Chicago's Far South is an area that merits a journey off the beaten tourist path. It encompasses the historic districts of Hyde Park and Kenwood, where you'll find magnificent architecture and stand-out museums, such as the DuSable Black History Museum and Education Center and the Griffin Museum of Science and Industry. Hyde Park and Kenwood both began life as suburbs for the wealthy escaping the city and even hosted the groundbreaking World's Columbian Exposition in 1893. Since then, this part of town has evolved and is now home to students of the University of Chicago and a vibrant mix of communities with Mexican, African, Asian, and Indian origins. Additionally, there are spectacular tracts of green space throughout this area, including the University of Chicago's Midway Plaisance and Jackson Park, site of the famous World's Columbian Exposition.**

*For places to stay in this area, see p121*

**Main campus of the University of Chicago**

## 1 University of Chicago

E6 5801 S. Ellis Ave. uchicago.edu

Noted for its research and high educational standards, this private university has produced over 80 Nobel Prize winning alumni and staff.

## 2 University of Chicago Sculptures

Over the years, the University of Chicago has acquired around 12 outdoor sculptures, including Wolf Vostell's playful 1970 *Concrete Traffic*, a car embedded in concrete at the southwest end of Midway Plaisance, and *Nuclear Energy*, a bronze sculpture by Henry Moore, that resembles a mushroom cloud. Within a reflecting pool at 60th Street and University Avenue is *Construction in Space in the Third and Fourth Dimension*, an abstract work created in the 1950s by Constructivist Antoine Pevsner. This striking piece depicts the space-time continuum.

## 3 Kenwood Historic District

E5

Bounded by East 43rd Street to the north and East 51st Street to the south, this wealthy enclave within Kenwood was founded by John A. Kennicott in 1856. In the late 19th century this area, which also stretches across South Blackstone Avenue to the east and South Drexel Boulevard to the west, was an upscale suburb, where residents built majestic homes on spacious lots, a rarity in the quickly booming city. A stroll around the district uncovers architectural styles ranging from Italianate and Colonial Revival to Prairie style, by influential figures such as Howard Van Doren Shaw and Frank Lloyd Wright.

## 4 Institute for the Study of Ancient Cultures

E6 1155 E. 58th St. 10am–4pm Tue–Sun (to 8pm Fri) isac.uchicago.edu

Learn about the origins of agriculture, writing, civilization, and the beginning of the study of arts, science, and religion at this University of Chicago museum. Five galleries showcase ancient Near Eastern civilizations from about 3500 BCE to 100 CE; most exhibits were unearthed during the department's own excavations.

**Sculpture at the Institute for the Study of Ancient Cultures**

Wright's Prairie School masterpiece, Robie House

## 5 Robie House

E6 5757 S. Woodlawn Ave. For tours: 10am–2:30pm Thu–Mon flwright.org/tour/robie-house

Frank Lloyd Wright's celebrated Robie House, easily identified by its steel-beam roof, served as a private residence until 1926, when it was converted into a dormitory. It was later bought by a development firm, who donated it to the University of Chicago in 1963, the same year it was designated a National Historic Landmark. Visitors can explore its low-ceilinged interior, and discover more about the decade-long restoration program.

## 6 Osaka Japanese Gardens

F6 6401 S. Stony Island Ave. Dawn–dusk daily

At the north end of Jackson Park's Wooded Island, lies this retreat, also known as the Garden of the Phoenix, which features meandering paths, lagoons, and fountains. The garden, a partial recreation of the original, was formed in 1934 around the Japanese Pavilion, which was built for the 1893 Exposition, but burned down in a fire in 1946. In 1993, the gardens were revitalized to honor Chicago's sister city, Osaka, which donated the Japanese gate seen here.

## 7 Griffin Museum of Science and Industry

The largest science museum *(p30)* within a single building in the Western Hemisphere, this popular museum attracts over two million people a year.

## 8 Washington Park

D5 5531 S. King Dr. Dawn–11pm daily

Frederick Law Olmsted and Calvert Vaux, the designers of New York's Central Park, also created this green space in the early 1870s. It originally attracted mainly wealthy city dwellers, but today, it is a widely used park with recreational programs, the DuSable Black History Museum and Education Center, and Lorado Taft's 110-ft (34-m) long sculpture, *Fountain of Time*, which took him 14 years to build.

Picturesque Osaka Japanese Gardens

## 9 DuSable Black History Museum and Education Center

D5 740 E. 56th Pl. 10am–5pm Tue–Sun dusablemuseum.org

Located on the eastern edge of Washington Park, this museum is named after Chicago's first non-native settler, Jean Baptiste Point du Sable. Its permanent exhibits celebrate other firsts, such as the first Black US astronaut, Major Robert Lawrence, and Chicago's first African American mayor, Harold Washington. Other thought-provoking exhibits include rusted shackles and the striking *Freedom Now* mural, depicting 400 years of African American history.

## 10 Stony Island Arts Bank

F6 6760 S. Stony Island Ave. 312-857-5561 Closed for renovation

In 2015, contemporary artist Theaster Gates, Jr., converted this 1893 bank into an exhibition and arts space, fostering gentrification in a region much in need of investment. The center houses the record collection of the late Chicago DJ Frankie Knuckles, considered the father of House music, and over 60,000 glass lantern slides from the art history department at the University of Chicago. Both collections can be seen during free tours every Saturday at 1pm.

### EXPLORING THE FAR SOUTH

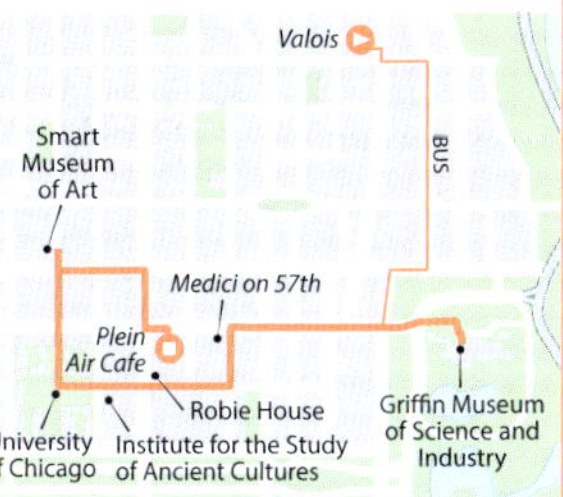


#### Morning

Start your day with a true South Side classic, the cafeteria **Valois** *(p107)*, which draws everyone from local pensioners to former President Obama. From there, walk about a mile (2 km) south or hop on the no. 28 bus at the corner of Hyde Park Boulevard and Lake Park Avenue to visit the **Griffin Museum of Science and Industry**, where you can explore the hands-on exhibits. For lunch, take a short walk west to **Medici on 57th** *(p107)*, a student and faculty hangout, known for its pizzas. Its extravagant Garbage Pizza is a local favorite.

#### Afternoon

Stroll about four blocks southwest to the **Institute for the Study of Ancient Cultures** *(p103)* at the **University of Chicago** *(p103)*. Its museum will transport you back to ancient times, and its Suq gift shop offers lovely souvenirs. Just east of the institute is Frank Lloyd Wright's masterpiece of Prairie-style architecture, **Robie House**. Take a tour of the house to gain some insight into the architect's vision. Then stroll around the university's grounds or backtrack a little to the **Smart Museum of Art** *(smartmuseum.uchicago.edu)*. Round off your day with a meal at **Plein Air Cafe** *(p107)* and enjoy the views of Robie House from its courtyard.

# Shopping

**1. Seminary Co-op Bookstore**
E6 5751 S. Woodlawn Ave.
Housed in the basement of the Chicago Theological Seminary on the University of Chicago campus, this bookstore has a well-respected academic section, especially humanities and social sciences.

**2. 57th Street Books**
E6 1301 E. 57th St.
This cozy basement shop, with its low ceilings, brick walls, and painted cement floor, is an ideal spot for browsing. It offers a wide selection of new adult fiction and children's books.

**3. Hyde Park Records**
E5 1377 E. 53rd St.
A favorite haunt of local musicians and a must-visit for touring DJs, Hyde Park Records specializes in vintage jazz, old soul, blues, gospel, and hip-hop records. Stop by its $1–$2 sale on the first Saturday of every month.

**4. Wesley's Shoe Corral**
F5 1506 E. 55th St
Celebrating more than 50 years in business, Wesley's is the oldest continuously operating Black-owned shoe store in the country. Men's, women's, and children's styles are sold with friendly service.

**5. Toys et Cetera**
F5 1502 E. 55th St.
This lovely store specializes in classic, old-fashioned toys, such as kites, balls, and face-painting kits. Unsurpisingly, it's a favorite among locals and families.

**6. Little Black Pearl Workshop**
C6 1060 E. 47th St.
The gift shop at this cultural arts center sells the students' creations, such as one-of-a-kind painted furniture and vibrant mosaics.

**Portraits on display at Kilimanjaro International**

**7. Sarah Kuenyefu Collection**
C6 4412 S. Cottage Grove Ave.
Mon
The scent of sandlewood incense fills this small boutique that sells African artifacts, apparel, carved wooden sculptures, and music albums from all over the continent.

**8. Silver Room**
F5 1506 E. 53rd St.
Founded in 1997, the Silver Room has been a go-to for locally designed apparel and accessories ever since. Its community-focused store also hosts events, such as talks and pop-up shops.

**9. Kilimanjaro International**
E5 1305 E. 53rd St.
Reflecting the local community's African roots, this fine arts and crafts specialty store features everything from jewelry to ceremonial masks.

**10. Powell's Books**
E6 1501 E. 57th St.
Here, used books in top condition are stacked floor to ceiling, with antique editions protected behind glass.

# Places to Eat

### 1. Cedars Mediterranean

E5 1206 E. 53rd St.
eatcedars.com · $

Cedars Mediterranean offers staples like falafel and chicken shawarma, plus tasty Mediterranean twists on wings and tacos.

**PRICE CATEGORIES**

Price categories include a three-course meal for one, a glass of house wine, tax, and a 15–20 percent tip.

$ under $30 $$ $30–$75 $$$ over $75

### 2. Valois

F5 1518 E. 53rd St.
valoisrestaurant.com · $

This cafeteria offers hearty meals such as roast beef and goulash. Note, only cash is accepted.

### 3. Dawn A.M. Eatery

F5 1642 E. 56th St.
dawnchi.com · $

A local favorite, Dawn A.M. is known for its Southern-inspired breakfasts – the waffles bites are a must-try.

### 4. Plein Air Cafe

E6 5751 S. Woodlawn Ave.
pleinaircafe.co · $

A charming café serving excellent coffee and European-influenced bites.

### 5. Harold's Chicken Shack

C5 Kimbark Plaza, 1208 E. 53rd St. haroldschickenhydepark.com · $

Enjoy fast soul food, including catfish and fried chicken with the famous Harold's Mild Sauce at this casual café.

### 6. Medici on 57th

E6 1327 E. 57th St.
medici57.com · $

Medici's pizzas attract a crowd, but sandwiches made with home-baked bread are just as tasty. Guests are welcome to bring their own liquor.

### 7. Virtue

F5 1462 E. 53rd St.
virtuerestaurant.com · $$

One of Hyde Park's few fine dining destinations, this chef-driven restaurant serves sumptuous Southern fare paired with wines and cocktails.

### 8. Woodlawn Tap

E5 1172 E. 55th St.
773-643-5516 · $

A casual atmosphere, good food, especially tasty burgers and sandwiches, and cheap beer attract locals and tourists alike to this bar.

### 9. Strugglebeard Bakery

F5 5221 S. Harper Ct.
strugglebeardbakery.com · $

Founded by a US Army veteran, this bakery serves excellent coffee and a variety of sweet treats, including its signature "Charles Anthony pecan and chocolate chunk cookie."

### 10. Chant

E5 1509 E. 53rd St.
chantchicago.com · $

With its funky vibe, unique cocktails, and global fusion cuisine, Chant is great at any time, but its Sunday brunch with live music is particularly good – and a real bargain.

**French atelier-inspired Plein Air Cafe**

# STREETSMART



*The "L" train in Downtown*

# GETTING AROUND

Whether exploring Chicago by foot or making use of public transportation, here is everything you need to know to navigate the city and the areas beyond the centre like a pro.

## AT A GLANCE

### PUBLIC TRANSPORTATION COSTS

Passes are valid on all CTA-operated public transportation options.

BUS
**$2.25**
Single bus journey

1-DAY PASSPORT
**$5.00**
Unlimited travel for one day

7-DAY PASSPORT
**$20.00**
Unlimited travel for seven days

### SPEED LIMIT

RURAL FREEWAYS
**65** mph (100 km/h)

URBAN FREEWAYS
**55** mph (90 km/h)

URBAN AREAS
**25** mph (40 km/h)

NEIGHBORHOOD SLOW ZONE
**20** mph (30 km/h)

## Arriving by Air

Most international and domestic flights arrive at **O'Hare International Airport**, located 20 miles (32 km) northwest of central Chicago. It's one of the world's busiest airports, serving most major international airlines, and has four terminals, with free transportation between them via the Airport Transport System (ATS) train. Do not be confused by the numbering of the terminals; there is no terminal 4 at O'Hare.

Chicago's second airport is **Midway International Airport**, 10 miles (16 km) southwest of downtown, which serves mostly domestic airlines. For a list of transportation options to both airports, see the table opposite.

**Midway International Airport**
W flychicago.com/midway

**O'Hare International Airport**
W flychicago.com/ohare

## Regional Trains

Up to 56 **Amtrak** trains serve Union Station in downtown each day, ranging from cross-country routes to a service to nearby Milwaukee. Reservations are necessary on many Amtrack routes and are advised during peak periods, such as the summer months and major holidays. Seats can be reserved online or in-person. Fares vary considerably based on advance purchase, with the cheapest fares for tickets bought at least 90 days ahead of travel.

Although Union Station is just west of the Loop and close to downtown Chicago, it's a good walk to hotels or CTA trains (the nearest "L" stop is at Clinton). If arriving in Chicago by train, it is probably best to plan on taking a taxi to your hotel; taxis are plentiful around the station.

**Amtrak**
W amtrak.com

## Long-Distance Bus Travel

The main terminal in Chicago for **Greyhound** Bus Line is a few blocks from

Union Station. It is not within easy walking distance to hotels in the Loop, so you may need to take a taxi to reach the station. Although walk-up ticket sales are readily available, Greyhound offers discounts for purchasing tickets online and in advance.

**Megabus** drops arrivals into Chicago directly oppposite Union Station and offers cheap regional transport between cities. Tickets must be booked online and are not sold by the driver or on the bus.

**Greyhound**
W greyhound.com

**Megabus**
W megabus.com

## Public Transportation

The Chicago Transit Authority (**CTA**) is Chicago's main public transportation authority. It runs Chicago's elevated train (the "L"as well as the city bus network. Security measures, timetables, ticket information, and transport maps can be obtained from the customer service office or the CTA website.

**CTA**
W transitchicago.com

### Tickets

**Ventra** is the fare payment system used on all CTA buses and trains, Metra trains, and Pace buses. Tickets and top-up cards can be purchased from ticket vending machines in "L" stations and select retailers around town (a list of these can be found on Ventra's website). Alternatively download the Ventra app and use a contactless payment system to tap-and-go on trains and buses.

Disposable tickets, with a pre-set value for a single ride or a day's travel, are best for a short stay, while the top-up card is recommended for longer stays. Ventra's top-up cards cost $5, but the fee is waived if you order the card online or refunded if you buy in person and register online within 90 days. Preload the card with credit, then use it each time you travel. Funds can be topped-up at ticket vending machines or by using the Ventra app.

Unlimited-ride passes for more than a day's travel can also be added to Ventra cards.

**Ventra**
W ventrachicago.com

### Local Trains

Short for elevated train, the "L" is the name given to the CTA train network, including the sections that travel underground. The eight lines covering the city's central districts are identifiable by color: red, green, blue, brown, orange, pink, purple, and yellow. Only the red and blue lines run 24 hours a day (less often off-peak). Trains arrive every 5 to 20 minutes, and CTA's smartphone app provides real-time schedules.

**Metra**, the commuter rail system, connects the suburbs with the city center. The 490-mile (790-km) system has 243 stations in the Illinois counties of Cook, Du Page, Lake, Will, McHenry, and Kane. It also services some cities in Indiana and Wisconsin. Trains run frequently during rush hour and every 1–3 hours at other times, and fares vary according to the journey's length.

**Metra**
W metra.com

### GETTING TO AND FROM THE AIRPORT

| Airport | Transport | Journey Time | Price |
|---|---|---|---|
| O'Hare International Airport | Taxi | 20-30 mins | $40 |
| | CTA Blue Line (L Train) | 40-45 mins | $5 |
| | Bus | 35-40 mins | $40 |
| Midway International Airport | Taxi | 20-40 mins | $25 |
| | CTA Orange Line (L train) | 20-25 mins | $2.50 |

## Buses

The CTA bus network covers the entire city and the suburbs, and is especially useful for reaching the lakefront, which is not served by the "L." Bus stops are indicated by blue- and white-stop signs.

Most buses run every 10–20 minutes from dawn to late evening daily. Night buses (indicated with an owl on the bus stop sign) run every 30 minutes 1am–4am daily. To board a bus, hail the driver and remain on the curb until the bus stops. Bike racks are located on the front of all CTA buses.

**PACE** buses, numbered 208 and higher, also ply the city suburbs. The PACE website has a live bus tracker, as well as timetables and bus route maps.

**PACE**
W pacebus.com

## Taxis

It is usually easy to hail a cab downtown and in popular neighborhoods; in residential districts, it's better to call for one. There's an initial charge, then a fee per mile and per extra passenger. A 10–15 percent tip is expected. There are several local cab companies and ride-sharing services such as Uber also operate in the city.

May through September, **Chicago Water Taxi** runs boats between the Wrigley Building and both the Union Station and the Ogilvie Transportation Center. **Shoreline Water Taxis** also offers a frequent river service to Willis Tower, as well as to popular attractions on Lake Michigan, such as Navy Pier and the Shedd Aquarium.

**Chicago Water Taxi**
W chicagowatertaxi.com
**Shoreline Water Taxis**
W shorelinesightseeing.com

## Driving

Driving in the city is not recommended for visitors. Parking can sometimes be difficult to find and is often expensive in the city center; plus, heavy traffic is common. Those traveling to Chicago by car are advised to leave their vehicle in a parking lot and use public transportation or taxis to get around.

Those arriving by car generally do so via the surrounding Interstate highways: I-55 from the southwest, I-57 from the south, I-88 from the west, I-90 from the east and northwest, and I-94 from the east and north. The legendary Route 66 from Santa Monica, California, joins I-55 before hitting the busy central streets of downtown Chicago.

## Car Rental

Rental car companies are located at both of Chicago's airports, major stations, and other locations in the city. Most companies will only rent cars to drivers 25 years and older with a valid driving license and clean record. All agencies require a major credit card. Damage and liability insurance is recommended just in case something unexpected should happen. Check your existing insurance policy before signing up to car insurance, as you may already be covered. It is advisable to always return the car with a full tank of gas, otherwise you will be required to pay an inflated fuel price.

A useful alternative to renting a vehicle is the car-share service **Zipcar**, which offers rentals by the hour or by the day. Members should apply online prior to reserving a car; charges include gas and insurance.

**Zipcar**
W zipcar.com

## Rules of the Road

The **Illinois Department of Transportation** website provides information on road closures and local weather conditions; it also features links to live traffic-incident maps.

Vehicles are driven on the right-hand side of the road in the US, except on one-way streets. You must wear a seatbelt, and it is illegal to talk on your mobile while driving. A right turn on a red light is permitted unless a sign prohibits it. Left turns are not allowed at some intersections during peak times, or are allowed only when the green arrow signal is illuminated.

As well as a maximum speed limit, the minimum speed regulation in Illinois means you could also be ticketed for driving too slowly. Tests and fines for drink driving are common in Illinois.

If you suffer a breakdown, call the American Automobile Association **(AAA)** for help.

**AAA**
W aaa.com
**Illinois Department of Transportation**
W idot.illinois.gov

### Parking

Street parking in Chicago falls into three categories: free, metered, and restricted. Downtown, free street parking is scarce and metered parking is the most readily available option.

Parking garages and lots in downtown Chicago are common but can be expensive. Outside of the central area, lots and garages are cheaper but harder to come by. Most are located around popular attractions like sports arenas and shopping districts.

In winter months, be careful not to park in snow emergency routes as your car may be towed.

## Cycling

Cycling is a popular form of transport in Chicago. There are more public bike racks in Chicago than any other city in the US, and more than 480 miles (770 km) of bike lanes – most major throughways have designated bike lanes. However, cyclists on the streets must still use extreme caution, obey traffic laws, and wear a safety helmet.

The lakefront offers 18 miles (29 km) of scenic paths, although it can be busy. Informal rules of the road exist, but it is often difficult for walkers, cyclists, and in-line skaters to co-exist. The best time to enjoy the path is during business hours when traffic is quieter.

The city encourages short commutes via bicycle with its bike-share service, **Divvy**. Riders can purchase a 24-hour pass for $18.10 at any of the hundreds of Divvy bike stations around the lakefront bike paths.

**Divvy**
W divvybikes.com

## Walking

The best way to explore Chicago, particularly the downtown and Northside areas (including the Magnificent Mile and Lincoln Park), is by walking. Many of these central sights are within easy walking distance of each other. Most of the streets in the central districts are relatively flat, so you won't have to tackle many hills when out and about.

As Chicago drivers can sometimes be aggressive, pedestrians should never solely rely on traffic lights; look both ways before crossing the street, and watch out for cars making right turns or racing through yellow lights.

## Guided Tours

Walking, coach, and boat tours with a guide are a great way to see the city. Sign-up with the Chicago Architecture Center (**CAC**) or **Chicago Detours** for tours of the Chicago's architecture, or discover a few of the city's local neighborhoods with **Chicago Neighborhood Tours** (Saturday's only). Alternatively, go it alone and try the **Chicago Trolley Company**; all-day hop-on, hop-off passes give you the freedom to do what you want.

Boat tour season is from April to October. Several companies offer Lake Michigan and Chicago River excursions. Lake cruises depart from Navy Pier, and river tours depart from the Michigan Avenue Bridge. Prices vary but many companies offer discounts when two or more tours per person are purchased.

**CAC**
W architecture.org
**Chicago Detours**
W chicagodetours.com
**Chicago Neighborhood Tours**
W chicagoneighborhoodtours.com
**Chicago Trolley Company**
W chicagotrolley.com

# PRACTICAL INFORMATION

A little local know-how goes a long way in Chicago. On these pages you can find all the essential advice and information you will need to make the most of your trip to this city.

**AT A GLANCE**

**CURRENCY**
US Dollar (USD)

**AVERAGE DAILY SPEND**

| SAVE | SPEND | SPLURGE |
|---|---|---|
| $150 | $250 | $350+ |

| BOTTLED WATER | COFFEE | BEER | DINNER FOR TWO |
|---|---|---|---|
| $2.50 | $3.50 | $7.00 | $90 |

**CLIMATE**

The longest days occur Jun–Aug. Nov–Feb sees the shortest daylight hours.

Temperatures average 74°F (23°C) in summer, and fall below freezing in winter.

The heaviest rainfall is during the summer, but showers (and regular winds) occur all year.

**ELECTRICITY SUPPLY**
The standard US electric current is 110 volts and 60 Hz. Power sockets are type A and B, fitting plugs with two flat pins.

## Passports and Visas

For entry requirements, including visas, consult your nearest US embassy or check the **US State Department** website. Canadians typically do not require a visa to enter the US, although there are some exceptions. Citizens of Australia, New Zealand, the UK, or the EU do not need a visa, but must apply in advance for the Electronic System for Travel Authorization (**ESTA**). There is a small charge for this service. All other visitors need to obtain a visa in advance of traveling. A return airline ticket is required to enter the country.

**ESTA**
W esta.cbp.dhs.gov
**US State Department**
W travel.state.gov

## Government Advice

Now more than ever, it is important to consult both your and the US government's advice before traveling. The US State Department, the UK Foreign, Commonwealth and Development Office (**FCDO**), and the **Australian Department of Foreign Affairs and Trade** offer the latest information on security, health, and local regulations.

**Australian Department of Foreign Affairs and Trade**
W smartraveller.gov.au
**FCDO**
W gov.uk/foreign-travel-advice

## Customs Information

You can find information on the laws relating to goods and currency taken in and out of the US on the **US Customs and Border Protection Agency** website. Passengers may carry $100 in gifts; 1 liter of alcohol as beer, wine, or liquor (if aged 21 years or older); 200 cigarettes, 100 cigars (not Cuban), or two kilograms (4.4 lbs) of smoking tobacco into the US without incurring tax.

**US Customs and Border Protection Agency**
W cbp.gov

## Insurance

We recommend that you take out a comprehensive insurance policy covering theft, loss of belongings, medical care, cancellations, and delays, and read the small print carefully. All medical and dental treatment is private and US health insurers do not have reciprocal arrangements, so it is important to take out medical insurance.

## Vaccinations

No inoculations are required to visit the US.

## Money

Most establishments accept major credit, debit, and prepaid currency cards. Contactless payments are widespread, and the Metropolitan Transportation Authority (MTA) has a contactless payment system on its subway and bus routes. Some smaller establishments that only accept cash will usually advertise this on their windows. ATMs are available throughout the city, though most banks charge for ATM use and currency exchange.

Banks may offer better exchange rates than the exchange windows at the airports, but rates vary and not all banks offer foreign exchanges.

At most restaurants, tipping is expected for waiters at 15–20 percent of the bill before taxes.

## Travelers with Specific Requirements

The majority of restaurants, hotels, shops, malls, and museums are accessible to wheelchair users. Many sidewalks have curb cuts that allow smooth passage when crossing the streets. All CTA buses and most train stations are also wheelchair accessible, with lifts and ramps.

The non-profit **Easy Access Chicago**'s website has help for travelers with specific requirements. The **Mayor's Office for People with Disabilities** provides services to residents with disabilities and details on city facilities. Museums and galleries such as the Art Institute of Chicago and the Griffin Museum of Science and Industry offer tours in American Sign Language and for those who are visually impaired.

**Easy Access Chicago**
W easyaccesschicago.org

**Mayor's Office for People with Disabilities**
W cityofchicago.org

## Language

The official language of Chicago is English, although you will hear multiple languages spoken across this cosmopolitan city.

## Opening Hours

Office hours for businesses are generally 9am–5pm Monday to Friday. Shop and mall hours can vary but they are usually open 10am–9pm Monday to Saturday and noon–5pm Sunday. The Northside boutiques and stores along the Magnificent Mile *(p40)* often stay open until 7 or 8pm every evening, except on Sundays.

Banks are usually open during regular office hours only, which is normally 9am–5pm Monday to Friday, though most banks offer 24-hour access to ATM machines.

The city's museums and attractions keep their own hours. Many extend their hours during the summer season and some offer at least one evening per week with extended opening hours. It is always best to consult their websites before visiting to avoid any disappointment.

Most banks, shops, offices, and attractions are closed for public holidays including Independence Day (Jul 4) and Thanksgiving (4th Thu in Nov).

Situations can change quickly and unexpectedly. Always check before visiting attractions and hospitality venues for up-to-date opening hours and booking requirements.

## Personal Security

Although much of Chicago is safe for visitors, there are areas where things can change on a block-by-block basis. Use common sense and be alert of your surroundings and you should enjoy a stress-free trip. As the most common crimes tourists encounter are pickpocketing and purse snatching, consider leaving your valuables in a safe place at your hotel.

If you have anything stolen, report the crime within 24 hours to the nearest police station and take ID with you. Get a copy of the crime report in order to claim on your insurance. Contact your embassy if you have your passport stolen, or in the event of a serious crime or accident.

As a rule, Chicagoans are very accepting of all people, regardless of their race, gender, or sexuality. The city has a long legacy of supporting the LGBTQ+ community: it was home to the first recognized gay rights organization in the US, the Society for Human Rights, and homosexuality was legalized in Illinois in 1962. Today it has the third-largest LGBTQ+ population in the US. Acceptance isn't always a given however, and if you do feel unsafe, the **Safe Space Alliance** pinpoints your nearest place of refuge.

**Safe Space Alliance**
W safespacealliance.com

## Health

The US has a world-class healthcare system and there are plenty of hospitals and emergency rooms in Chicago. Treatment can be very expensive and payment of hospital and other medical expenses is the patient's responsibility. As such it is important to arrange comprehensive medical insurance before you travel and inform your insurer if you receive any treatment. Keep receipts to make a claim on your insurance.

Pharmacies are plentiful across the city. Many drug stores are open 24 hours and some of the more popular drug store chains, including **Walgreens** and **CVS**, have pharmacies inside. The pharmacies in 24-hour drug stores are usually only open during regular business hours and often close on Sunday. Some dental clinics are open 24 hours for emergency procedures. Check with your hotel or contact the **Chicago Dental Society** for a referral.

### AT A GLANCE

**EMERGENCY NUMBERS**

GENERAL EMERGENCY
**911**

**TIME ZONE**
CST/CDT
Central Daylight Time (CDT) runs from the second Sunday in Mar-early Nov.

**TAP WATER**
Unless otherwise stated, tap water is safe to drink.

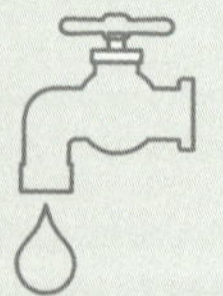

**WEBSITES AND APPS**

**Choose Chicago**
The city's tourism website (and app) provides detailed visitor information, attraction listings, and deals for travelers *(choosechicago.com)*.

**Ventra**
This app allows users to store transit passes and book tickets for the CTA ("L"), Metra trains and Pace buses.

**Divvy Bikes**
Chicago's bike sharing system has over 17,000 bikes and 950 docking stations, with both a website *(p113)* and app through which you can reserve a bike.

**Parknow**
Book parking spaces in advance, or find open parking spaces in the city.

**Chicago Dental Society**
W cds.org
**CVS**
W cvs.com
**Walgreens**
W walgreens.com

## Smoking, Alcohol, and Drugs

The legal minimum age for drinking alcohol in the US is 21, and you will need photo ID as proof of age in order to purchase alcohol and be allowed into bars. It is illegal to drink alcohol in public parks or to carry an open container of alcohol in your car. The US has a strict limit of 0.08 percent blood alcohol for drivers, which is strictly enforced, and penalties for driving under the influence of alcohol are severe.

Smoking is prohibited in all public buildings, bars, restaurants, and stores. Cigarettes can be purchased by those over 21 years old with ID.

Other than marijuana, which is legal in Illinois, narcotics are prohibted and can result in a prison sentence.

## ID

It is not compulsory to carry ID at all times. If you are asked by police to show your ID, a photocopy of your passport photo page should suffice. You may be asked to present the original document within 12 or 24 hours.

## Responsible Travel

Chicago is committed to reducing its footprint by 62 percent by 2040, and there are simple ways visitors can help toward these goals. Reduce emissions by using the city's public transportation system *(p111)*, or by walking and cycling around the city – this is one of the most bike-friendly cities in the US with a well-run bike-sharing program, Divvy *(p113)*. Visitors can also embrace locally and sustainably sourced cuisine at farm-to-table restaurants and the city's many farmers' markets. Additionally, make use of the public water fountains when exploring and use reusable water bottles and bags when out and about.

## Cell Phones and Wi-Fi

The City of Chicago offers free Wi-Fi hotspots around the city, including all 80 Chicago Public Libraries and some other public sites. Many cafes and restaurants will let you use their Wi-Fi, providing you make a purchase.

Chicago has two area codes: 312 for downtown and the immediate vicinity, and 773 for the rest of the city, including the Northside and South Side. Most cell phones work in America if unlocked by your carrier. Check the costs before you travel, or consider buying a local SIM card to avoid high roaming costs.

## Post

Most branches of the **US Postal Service** are open 9am–6pm Monday to Friday and 9am–1pm Saturday. Stamps can be bought from post offices, drug stores, and newsstands. On-street mailboxes are navy blue and are available on many street corners.

**US Postal Service**
W usps.com

## Taxes and Refunds

Chicago state and local sales taxes are among the highest in the country at 10.25 percent on all non-food items. In addition to any tip, taxes will add 10.7 percent to your food bill.

## Discount Cards

For discounted admission to a number of worthwhile tours and sites (including some museums), look for the **Go Chicago Card** and the **Chicago City Pass**. The Go Chicago Card provides access to 28 different tours and sites, and costs $114 (subject to change) for a 1-day pass and $239 for a 5-day pass (with reductions for children). The Chicago City Pass costs $134 ($104 for children) and is valid for nine days. Both cards can be bought at tourist centers as well as major must-see sites.

**Chicago City Pass**
W citypass.com/chicago
**Go Chicago Card**
W smartdestinations.com/chicago

# PLACES TO STAY

Chicago is home to some of America's best accomodations, with options for every budget range, from luxury hotels to more affordable hostels. The Loop and the Near North are the city's premier tourist districts and offer by far the most choice in terms of hotels.

You'll find the cheapest rates from November to March (thanks to the cold and snow) while summer tends to be the most expensive period. Room rates are usually quoted without taxes (21–24 percent in Chicago) and the "destination" fee at some top hotels.

**PRICE CATEGORIES**

For a standard, double room per night (with breakfast if included), taxes, and extra charges.

$ under $200
$$ $200–$400
$$$ over $400

## The Loop

### Chicago Athletic Association

**L4 12 S Michigan Ave chicagoathletichotel.com · $$**

Don't let the reasonable price fool you, this former members-only club still retains a sense of exclusivity. The building has a sumptuous Venetian Gothic design and perks that include the Game Room bar (in the former billiards room), Cindy's rooftop bar, free entry to the ground-floor golf simulator, and the on-site Shake Shack, which is part of the room service.

### The Fairmont Chicago

**L3 200 N Columbus Dr fairmontchicago.com · $$$**

Expect old-school luxury at this branch of the five-star Fairmont chain. The hotel has 686 rooms, all with bespoke furnishings and views of the city skyline or Lake Michigan. If that isn't enough, there are also luxurious treatment options at the on-site Leaf Spa and world-class Latin American fare at the Toro Chicago restaurant, run by celebrity chef Richard Sandoval.

### HI Chicago (The J. Ira and Nicki Harris Family Hostel)

**K5 24 E. Ida B. Wells Drive hiusa.org · $**

If you need a central spot that's budget-friendly, HI Chicago is the place for you. It's just steps away from sites such as Grant Park and the Art Institute of Chicago, and has all the important hostel amenities: free Wi-Fi, large common lounge, a well-stocked kitchen, and a games room.

### Kimpton Gray

**K4 122 W Monroe St grayhotelchicago.com · $$$**

The Kimpton has everything you could need for a fully restorative stay. It's like a fancy resort: there are Peloton classes, yoga mats in every room, free bikes, scooters for kids, meditation pods in the wellness lounge, and a nightly social hour. Best of all, the Kimpton uses environmental practices.

### L7 Chicago by Lotte

**L3 225 N Wabash Ave l7chicago.com · $**

L7 is the place that proves luxury in the Loop doesn't have to break the bank. It can match most higher-priced hotels with its list of amenities, which include Korean skincare products and exercise equipment in the rooms, and has a world-class on-site steak house, serving inventive twists on Korean BBQ dishes.

### Nobu Hotel Chicago

**H4 155 N Peoria St nobuhotels.com · $$$**

If you're after a foodie stay, look no further than Nobu. The hotel was set up by lauded chef, Nobu Matsuhisa, and has two fabulous eateries – on the ground floor and the rooftop – where you can try some of his famous dishes. But if you do want something other than the Nobu fare, Chicago's famed Restaurant Row is just a stone's throw away.

### Pendry Chicago

L3 230 N Michigan Ave pendry.com · $$$

Architecture lovers, this Art Deco landmark is for you. The Pendry is set within the 1929 Carbide & Carbon Building, built to look like "a dark green champagne bottle with gold foil at the top." It became a hotel in 2004 and the rooms now blend 1920s design and contemporary touches (think MiN New York amenities and Bluetooth speakers).

### Publishing House B&B

G4 108 N May St publishinghousebnb.com · $

Few buildings in Chicago have a more interesting history than this place. The 1909 building has been a Methodist publishing house, a casket factory, and holographry museum. It's now a B&B with nods to its varied past throughout; original wood paneling, maple floors, 1980s holograms, and rooms named after a local author or a Chicago-set novel, with copies of the relevant work, inside.

### St. Regis Chicago

L3 401 E Wacker Dr marriott.com · $$$

The St. Regis opened here in 2023 and has certainly lived up to the brand's reputation for luxury. Expect all the usual bells and whistles: signature butler service, afternoon and evening tea "rituals," a wellness floor with a huge pool, and award-winning eateries like the Tuscan-inspired Tre Dita. On top of it all, the St. Regis has jawdropping lakefront views.

## Near North

### Freehand Chicago

K3 19 E Ohio St freehandhotels.com · $

In a district packed with big-budget hotels, the Freehand is a welcome budget-friendly option. The 1927 building has a mix of hostel-style four-bunk dorms and ensuite private rooms, decorated with kitsch items and art by Bard College students. Better yet, there's an award-winning cocktail bar, Broken Shaker, the perfect place to socialize in the evenings.

### Four Seasons Hotel Chicago

L2 120 E Delaware Pl fourseasons.com · $$$

The grand dame of Chicago luxury hotels has all the amenities you'd expect of a top-tier hotel (full-service spa, large indoor pool, and refined restaurant). But its real selling point is the location, right on the Magnificent Mile (there's even a Bloomingdale's department store in the tower).

### The Gwen

L3 521 N Rush St thegwenchicago.com · $$$

The Gwen, situated in the historic 1929 McGraw-Hill Building, is all about (luxurious) fun. There's the Tipsy Tea Party on Saturdays, with DJ sets and bottomless drinks; live jazz shows on Wine Wednesdays, and even a Moët & Chandon champagne vending machine. The Gwen hosts art exhibitions and fun-filled craft evenings, too, and has bicycles that guests can rent, for free.

### Hotel EMC2

L2 228 E Ontario St hotelemc2.com· $$

Live out your modern tech fantasies at this quirky Streeterville hotel. All rooms have their own Amazon Alexa, two robot attendants (Cleo and Leo) to see to your every need, and a horn-shaped gramophone amplifier, which you can plug your phone into. Fans of old technology should check out the historic zoetrope (a primitive 19th-century animation device) found in the lobby.

### InterContinental Chicago Magnificent Mile

L3 505 N Michigan Ave ihg.com · $$$

What makes this luxury hotel so great? It could be the incredible 1920s architecture (the hotel was originally part of the Medinah Athletic Club). It could be the huge pool with its stadium seating and Spanish majolica tiles. Or perhaps it's the great restaurants, which includes Michael Jordan's Steak House. Book in and decide yourself.

### The Langham, Chicago

K3 330 N Wabash Ave
langhamhotels.com · $$$

The elegant design of the Langham makes it stand out from the crowd. The tower was the last crafted by architect Mies van der Rohe and features his signature touches, ranging from travertine bathroom walls to floor-to-ceiling windows in every room. These have been enhanced by marble surfaces, an extensive collection of art, and cozy armchairs, and chaise longues to enjoy the view.

### The Peninsula Chicago

L2 108 E Superior St
peninsula.com · $$$

After a one-of-a-kind hotel? Then book a stay here. This branch of the luxury chain has the only hotel ice-skating rink in Chicago, and best of all it's on the rooftop terrace, with fantastic views. You'll feel even better knowing the hotel has eliminated single-use plastics, is EarthCheck certified, and is working to reduce its carbon footprint by 55 percent by 2030.

### Ohio House Motel

K3 600 N La Salle Dr
ohiohousemotel.com · $

If you love a bit of old-school Americana, check out this gem that's been a city staple since 1960. The simple rooms have retained a mid-century feel in line with the futuristic Googie architecture, that was so ubiquitous in postwar America. But don't think the motel is dated: it has all the mod-cons you need, including big TVs and free Wi-Fi.

### Waldorf Astoria Chicago

K2 11 E Walton St
hilton.com · $$$

It's easy to think you're in Europe, rather than the Midwest, when staying at the Waldorf. There's the large Parisian-style courtyard and equally Parisian decor in the rooms, handcrafted English beds, and elegant marble that's reminiscent of a historic European palace. You'll even have access to the hotel's fleet of Audi cars to get around town.

## Northside

### Longman & Eagle

B4 2657 N Kedzie Ave
longmanandeagle.com · $

Hipster vibes reign at this cool lodging – picture a rope-hung terrarium, vintage cassettes, and plenty of well-thumbed books around the place. Better yet, with only six rooms you can expect high-quality service, not to mention top-notch food and drink from the Bib Gourmand-awarded gastropub, located below the hotel.

### Villa D'Citta

B4 2230 N Halsted St
villadcitta.com · $$

Packed full of old world charm, Villa D'Citta is a piece of Italy in the heart of Chicago. The renovated 19th-century building features marble fireplaces, hardwood floors, and grandiose furniture that evokes the home of an Italian count. There are also neat touches like antique maps of Italy and portraits on the walls. Guests have access to the kitchen, which is always stocked with food.

### The Guesthouse Hotel

B3 4872 N Clark St
theguesthousehotel.com · $$

You won't lack for space at this place, located between Uptown and the historically Swedish Andersonville area. You can choose from big one-, two-, or three-bedroom suites, all kitted out for long stays with full-size kitchens, separate living areas, and balconies. You can even meet your fellow guests at the club room or the library (with books you can also borrow).

### The Neighborhood Hotel

E3 2616 N Clark St
theneighborhoodhotel.com · $$

The best thing about this hotel? Its location, right at the northern end of Lincoln Park, close to many shops and restaurants. It's perfect for anyone who wants to explore the beaches on Lake Michigan's shoreline. The 14 stylish and thoroughly modern apartments are also a draw, with fully stocked kitchens, comfy furnishings, and nice touches such as yoga mats and Moccamaster coffee machines.

### The Robey

B4 2018 W North Ave therobey.com · $$

Housed in a 1920s Art Deco tower, this hotel certainly has a historic feel to it. But inside it's a different story, thanks to a look that mixes retro touches with modern minimalism. The building is the only high-rise in the area, meaning it has sensational views, and a rooftop bar to boot.

### Stay 424 Hostel

D4 1415 N Ashland Ave stay424hostel.com · $

Digital nomads, this one's for you. The 424 has everything needed for a good day's work, from a well-equipped coworking space to studios for both podcasting and photography. Once the working day is done, head up to the rooftop to socialize with your fellow nomads on the rooftop deck.

### Wrigley Hostel – Chicago

E1 3514 N Sheffield Ave wrigleyhostel.com · $

If you're a social butterfly, book a stay at this hostel. It's packed with activities, such as a pool table, dartboard, board games, and a grill for BBQs. Furthermore, it's a short stroll from the hotel to the many fun nightlife spots on Clark Street and the famous LGBTQ+-friendly bars of Northalsted.

### Hotel Zachary

D1 3630 N Clark St hotelzachary.com · $$

This is the place to stay if you're a baseball fan. The hotel is opposite Wrigley Field, where the Chicago Cubs have played since 1916, making it the most convenient location for fans attending a game. Rooms feature floor-to-ceiling windows, and suites have balconies, all overlooking the ballpark.

## South Loop

### The Blackstone

L5 636 S Michigan Ave theblackstonehotel.com · $$

They don't make 'em like this anymore. This huge hotel opened in 1910 and is a Beaux Arts masterpiece. Though the hotel has since been renovated to add modern amenities, it still retains the vintage lobby, historic ballroom, and many of its original detailings. It's no wonder that 12 US presidents have stayed here.

### Marriott Marquis Chicago

C5 2121 S Prairie Ave marriott.com · $$$

Business or leisure? Both are catered for at this modern high-rise hotel. It's connected via a skybridge to the McCormick Place, the largest convention center in the US. As for the leisure, the sites of the Museum Campus are within easy reach of the hotel, as is the historic NFL stadium, Soldier Field.

### SpringHill Suites Chicago Chinatown

E5 2357 S Wentworth Ave marriott.com · $$

As the name implies, the selling point of this all-suite hotel is its location, right in the middle of the city's Chinatown. As such, the hotel is near to the best Chinese food in the city, which you can enjoy while exploring the traditional Chinese architecture on show here.

## Far South

### SOPHY Hyde Park

E5 1411 E 53rd St sophyhotel.com · $$$

Expect Southside cool in this 2018 addition to Hyde Park's hotel scene. Rooms all have record players, with complimentary vinyl, and are decorated in bold colors and abstract paintings by local artist Joey Korom. The walls in the rest of the hotel are adorned by 60 original works of art by students from a local high school.

### The Study at the University of Chicago

E6 1227 E 60th St thestudyatuniversityofchicago.com · $$

If you want to be close to the University of Chicago, this is the best option – the Study overlooks Midway Plaisance Park near the campus and has 167 cozy rooms. Relax with a book by the fireplace in the living room and enjoy a meal in the on-site tavern, which serves British pub grub.

# INDEX

Page numbers in **bold** refer to main entries

# ACKNOWLEDGMENTS


## This edition updated by

**Contributors** Stephen Keeling, Nicole Schnitzler

**Senior Editors** Keith Drew, Kiron Gill, Alison McGill

**Senior Designer** Vinita Venugopal

**Project Editor** Charlie Baker

**Editors** Ilina Choudhary, Abhidha Lakhera, Pankhoori Sinha

**Proofreaders** Ben Ffrancon Downds, Ruth Reisenberger

**Indexer** Hilary Bird

**Deputy Picture Research Manager** Virien Chopra

**Assistant Picture Research Administrator** Manpreet Kaur

**Rights and Permissions Specialist** Priya Singh

**Publishing Assistant** Simona Velikova

**Jacket Designers** Katie Cavanagh, Vinita Venugopal

**Jacket Picture Researcher** Diana Jarvis

**Senior Cartographer** Subhashree Bharati

**Senior Cartographic Editor** James Macdonald

**Cartography Manager** Suresh Kumar

**Pre-Production Coordinator** Tanveer Zaidi

**Pre-Production Designer** Rohit Rojal

**Pre-Production Image Coordinator** Jagtar Singh

**Pre-Production Image Editor** Vikram Singh

**Pre-Production Manager** Balwant Singh

**Pre-Production Image Manager** Pankaj Sharma

**Senior Production Controller** Samantha Cross

**Deputy Managing Editor** Dharini Ganesh

**Managing Editor** Beverly Smart

**Managing Art Editor** Gemma Doyle

**Senior Managing Art Editor** Priyanka Thakur

**Editorial Director** Hollie Teague

**Art Director** Maxine Pedliham

**Publishing Director** Georgina Dee

DK would like to thank the following for their contribution to the previous editions: Rohan Bolton, Elaine Glusac, Susanne Hillen, Elisa Kronish, Lauren Viera, Sotonoff.

The publisher would like to thank the following for their kind permission to reproduce their photographs:

(Key: a-above; b-below/bottom; c-centre; f-far; l-left; r-right; t-top)

**Adobe Stock:** ezellhphotography 30; nejdetduzen 56; Brad Pict 21cr, 43b; Dian Liu / Wirestock Creators 36–37t.

**Alamy Stock Photo:** ANP 10bl; AP Photo / Charles Rex Arbogast 37b; Edwin Baker 64; Todd Bannor 38cb, 38bl, 101; Georg Berg 41t, 67b; Dalibor Brlek 12cra; Chicago History Museum 10tl; Felix Choo 89t; Chronicle of World History 10br; Serhii Chrucky 13cl (8), 98–99b; CNMages 100; Ian Dagnall 68–69b, 83; Ian G Dagnall 35t; Orjan Ellingvag 11; Richard Ellis 38br; EmmePi Images 17; Entertainment Pictures 52t; EQRoy 87; Jeremy Graham 15br; GRANGER - Historical Picture Archive 9tl; Allan Hartley 15bl, 21tr; Peter J. Hatcher 8; Spiekermeier Francoise / Hemis.fr 94; History and Art Collection 33t; Roy Johnson 45; Gina Kelly 51b; Jon Lovette 13cla, 42b; mauritius images GmbH / Rupert Oberhäuser 80; Doug McGoldrick 47; Simon Montgomery 25; National Geographic Image Collection / Richard Nowitz 84; Niday Picture Library 9br; Panther Media Global / RM45 89b; PF-(bygone1) 33b; Lana Rastro 51t; Rich Kane Photography 10cl; robertharding / Amanda Hall 91; RooM the Agency / darekm101 65b; Philip Scalia 44; Science History Images / Photo Researchers 9cr, 49t; Helen Sessions 86; Stars and Stripes 40cra; Dawid Swierczek 31bl; Tribune Content Agency LLC / McClatchy-Tribune 92; Universal Images Group North America LLC / Jumping Rocks 58; Michael Ventura 26t; David Vilaplana 81; Jim West 57; Westend61 GmbH 41b; Wang Ping / Xinhua 71; H. Rick Bamman / ZUMA Press Wire 61t; ZUMA Press / Karen I. Hirsch 13clb.

**The Art Institute of Chicago:** Edward Hopper, American, 1882-1967. *Nighthawks*, 1942. Oil on canvas. 33 1/8 x 60 in. (84.1 x 152.4 cm). Friends of American Art Collection 24cla; Pierre Auguste Renoir, French, 1841-1919. Two Sisters (*On the Terrace*), 1881. Oil on canvas. 39 9/16 x 37 7/8 in. (100.5 x 81 cm) The Art Institute of Chicago, Mr. and Mrs. Lewis Larned Coburn Memorial

Collection 26b; Grant Wood, American, 1891-1942. American Gothic, 1930. Friends of American Art Collection. 24br.

**AWL Images:** Susanne Kremer 6–7.

**Chicago Shakespeare Theater:** James Steinkamp 62.

**Choose Chicago:** Adam Alexander Photography 75b; City of Chicago 90.

**Dreamstime.com:** 4kclips 9cra; Mohamed Abdelrazek 15cb; Amadeustx 34–35b; Alexander Cimbal 79; Ellesi 63; F11photo 54; Filedimage 65t; Christian Heinz 61b; Joe Hendrickson 14, 16tl, 23tl; Christian Hinkle 76; Chon Kit Leong 42–43t; Maisna 68t; Sean Pavone 78; Rosana Scapinello 48; Roman Slavik 109; Spiroview Inc. 20; Theresasc75 98t; Xbrchx 16cra; Zachary Zuchowski 27.

**Edible Ink PR:** Stronghold Photography / Neil John Burger 93.

© **Field Museum:** 29br; Lucy Hewett 16cl; Michelle Kuo 28–29b; Greg Neise 29t.

**Getty Images:** Tim Boyle / Bloomberg 22; E. Jason Wambsgans / Chicago Tribune / Tribune News Service 106. Moment Open / by Ken Ilio 12cr; Melissa Tamez / NBAE 13tl; The Image Bank / Bob Krist 19; The Image Bank Unreleased / Jon Hicks 67t; The Image Bank Unreleased / Maremagnum 66; Daniel Boczarski / Stringer 13cl.

**Getty Images / iStock:** benedek 40b, 103t; Thomas Campone 70; dibrova 52b; E+ / rudisill 12br; E+ / tunart 12crb; E+ / xavierarnau 49b; lucky-photographer 23ca; Ionel Łupu 1; Nicola Patterson 23tr; Jeremy Poland 85; stevegeer 38clb.

**Museum of Science and Industry, Chicago, Il:** 31br, 32; J.B. Spector 31cb.

**North Pond Restaurant:** 95.

**Plein Air Cafe:** Nathan Michael Gomez (nathanmichaeldesign.com) 107.

**Shutterstock.com:** Jonah Anderson 104–105b; ChicagoPhotographer 36b, 103b; CK Foto 13bl; EQRoy 21clb, 104t; JTTucker 60; Kit Leong 97; Moses P 5; Arthur Paley 39; Paramount / Everett 53; STLJB 75t; Rajesh Vijayakumar 59; Kamil Zelezik 73; zhongyugan 55.

## Cover Images:

*Front and Spine:* **4Corners:** Massimo Borchi / Studio Gang.

*Back:* **Adobe Stock:** Brad Pict tr; **Getty Images / iStock:** lucky-photographer tl, Jeremy Poland cl.

## Sheet Map Cover Image:

**4Corners:** Massimo Borchi / Studio Gang.

**Illustrator:** Lee Redmond.

**A NOTE FROM DK**

The rate at which the world is changing is constantly keeping the DK travel team on our toes. While we've worked hard to ensure that this edition of Chicago is accurate and up-to-date, we know that opening hours alter, standards shift, prices fluctuate, places close and new ones pop up in their stead. So, if you notice we've got something wrong or left something out, we want to hear about it. Please get in touch at travelguides@dk.com

Within each Top 10 list in this book, no hierarchy of quality or popularity is implied. All 10 are, in the editor's opinion, of roughly equal merit.

First edition 2004

Published in Great Britain by Dorling Kindersley Limited, DK, 20 Vauxhall Bridge Road, London SW1V 2SA

The authorised representative in the EEA is Dorling Kindersley Verlag GmbH. Arnulfstr. 124, 80636 Munich, Germany

Published in the United States by DK Publishing, 1745 Broadway, 20th Floor, New York, NY 10019, USA



26 27 28 29 10 9 8 7 6 5 4 3 2 1



A CIP catalog record for this book is available from the British Library.

A catalog record for this book is available from the Library of Congress.

ISSN: 1479-344X
ISBN: 978 0 2417 8331 3

Printed and bound in China

**www.dk.com**

This book was made with Forest Stewardship Council™ certified paper – one small step in DK's commitment to a sustainable future.

Learn more at **www.dk.com/uk/information/sustainability**